Another Bump I.. ....─ ...

**An Incomplete Traveller's Guide To
Southern Europe, Western Asia,
North Africa, Turkey, The 'Stans',
And The Silk Road To The East.**

Introduction:

This book was inspired by the author's own plans for travelling to countries on the far eastern reaches of Europe and into Asia - 'The Stans'.

We have also drawn from an enjoyment of travelling through North Africa, Morocco and Southern Europe.

Therefore the routes and more detailed information on countries are more specific when referring to those on the silk road, around that area, Southern Europe and North Africa - quite a wide spectrum.

Our suggested routes throughout, are aimed as a guide towards the east, as a traveller journeying from the U.K. through France and Italy, down to Greece or through Turkey to Georgia, the surrounding states in Asia and also travelling south, from the U.K. through France, Spain and into Morocco.

There are, however, very pertinent and useful tips and tricks and guides to many European and North African countries as well, which we hope to add to in the near future, so watch out for new additions.

We have listed accommodation costs only where these are significantly different to the rest of the world.

There have been many and varied books and websites aimed at the tourist and traveller giving detailed information on places of interest - we are awash with detail.

For this reason we have not gone into too much depth as far as the more frequent destinations are concerned but simply listed them as per country and concentrated on the more 'out of the way' interests and destinations 'less travelled'.

Where we have listed places of interest, these have been compiled mostly in order of a route map rather than simply a list of places to go, but, whether these routes work for your own particular journey we could not advise.
Feel free to adapt for your own purposes.

There are always more places of interest, essential things to know, items to take, personal loves and hates, etc. that may be missing from a travel guide such as this one.

For this reason we have left blank pages with each section, for you to add your own delights and 'need to know' information.

This will become your own travelogue.

In many ways the surprise factor, the things that happen when travelling, that are not expected, are the very things that create an enjoyable and exciting experience - these are the times that memories are made of

Please, let us know your own 'special places' and anything that you feel would be a useful addition to this book and we will be pleased to add them in, with a mention of your written donation.

Life, especially life on the road, journeying, is a shared experience, we are a community of travellers, it is the journey, both on the road and the decisions that we make through life, that will decide our future.

Enjoy this contribution and please, never be afraid to encounter the unexpected.

Some of the information found within these pages will apply only to the U.K. resident.

Please make enquiries of your own with regards to nation specific information.

From Europe moving into Asia:

Required and Useful:

This book.

A 1968 International Driving Permit (IDP).

Travel insurance in case paperwork is lost.

Travel insurance is available at a discount through against the compass.com

For driving through many countries, particularly within the E.U. you will need:

Snow chains.

Two standard yellow warning triangles.

A U.K. sticker on the rear of your vehicle or incorporated within your number plate (Not a G.B. sticker).

Several passport sized photos to use with documents you may need to collect during your journey.

Transit visas - required in certain countries.

U.S. dollars. - Many traders and businesses will accept U.S. dollars or Euros, sometimes in preference to their own currency.

Instead of converting physical banknotes, the cheapest way to pay in most countries is to use a multi-currency travel debit card like **Revolut** or **Wise.**

Road and terrain maps, of each country being visited, are useful as wifi may be scarce, particularly when travelling through the country and mountainside.

Guide books from lonelyplanet.com - these are the best for using in eastern Europe.

A good set of Binoculars.

Useful phrase book.

First aid and Medical necessities.

Water purification - tablets or other means of water purification.

Things to Remember:

Check out credit and cash card suppliers that offer low or nil percent commission on international cash transactions and withdrawals.

Travel insurance.

Vehicle breakdown insurance pertinent to the countries you are visiting.

Do you need a new passport?
Some countries require a minimum of six months unexpired on a passport.

Polio, yellow fever, typhoid and any other necessary vaccinations.

Visas and e visas

Mosquito net for car or van

Personal mosquito net

It would be wise to photocopy important documents and store them in the cloud.
Keep a list of passwords separately.

Mobile phone
Mobile phone charger

Laptop
Laptop charger

We have found that buying a local sim card and/or a
dongle is the best way to stay online and locateable, but
this is not always reliable when travelling through the
countryside.

Continental Electrical Socket Adapters/Converters.

A good torch.

Box of matches.

Can opener.

Bottle opener

Necessary:

Money

Passport

Driving licence

Car insurance

Green card

International driving permit. - 1968 obtained from the post office over the counter - cost: £5.50. and lasts three years.

Headlamp diverters

Two Road Breakdown triangles

A Full Set of Vehicle Bulbs.

Hi vis vest.

Schengen info:

Applicable mainly to U.K. residents:

If the 90 day limit is exceeded you will be given 30 days to exit the zone.
No fines are expected at the time of going to print..

There are new **ETIAS** rules with regards to travel within **The European Union** coming into play during 2024 so keep a watchful eye on these new rules.

Countries in the E.U. that are non Schengen:

Bulgaria
Cyprus
Ireland
Romania
Switzerland
Iceland
Norway

Countries not in the E.U. who are non Schengen:

All countries within the U.K.
Moldova
Belarus
Albania
Ukraine
Bosnia & Herzegovina
Azerbaijan

Serbia
Lichtenstein
Macedonia
Montenegro
Turkey
Vatican City
Russia
San Marino
Monaco
Kosovo
Andorra
Holy See

Countries with membership in the European Union:

Austria, Belgium, Bulgaria, Croatia, Republic of Cyprus,
Czech Republic, Denmark, Estonia, Finland, France,
Germany, Greece, Hungary, Ireland, Italy, Latvia,
Lithuania, Luxembourg, Malta, Netherlands, Poland,
Portugal, Romania, Slovakia, Slovenia, Spain and
Sweden.

Useful Websites:

Againstthecompass.com - Excellent guides, tips and itineraries

Bordercrossingscaravanistan.com - useful notes on whether borders are open or not.

Journalofnomads.com

https://www.getyourguide.co.uk - local city guides.

Lonelyplanet.com

Travellemming.com

Landcruisingadventure.com

Visagenie.co.uk - helpful visa application

Caravanistan.com
Caravanistan.com can also help with visas that are stuck or delayed.

Border crossing map:

https://www.google.com/maps/d/u/0/viewer?mid=1Ml8xr hk9Jwr00_GdccYtBrEYScU&ll=44.09191269522799%2 C67.36244529986926&z=5

Fuel:

It is approx 5000 miles from London, U.K. to Samarkand in Uzbekistan.
Total cost: @ 20p per mile - £1,000.00.

In Europe diesel is known as gasoil, gasol, gaz-oil, gasolio, gasóleo, dieselolie, mazot, motorina, nafta, or just plain diesel.

Gasoline Type Fuels:

Petrol: - Marked by an "E" inside a circle: E5, E10, etc. "E" stands for specific bio-components (ethanol) present in petrol.

Copyright and Source European Committee for Standardization

Diesel Type Fuels:

Marked by a "B" inside a square: B7, B10, XTL, etc "B" stands for specific biodiesel components present in diesel, the XTL stands for synthetic diesel and indicates that it is not derived from crude oil.

B7 is ok for all diesel vehicles
B10 is not ok for all, but is ok for some.

Spain:

Pay extra attention in Spain, where gasoline (petrol) is gasolina and diesel is sometimes called gasóleo.

France:
In France petrol is called 'sans plomb'
Diesel is called diesel.
Traditionally in France petrol pumps have been green and diesel have been yellow.

Italy:
It is benzina (petrol) and gasolio (diesel).

Greece:
Petrol is called "unleaded benzine".
Beware because petrol sounds a lot like 'petreleo' which is what diesel is called in **Greece.**

Turkey:
Diesel is called motorin and unleaded is kurşunsuz benzin.

Morocco:
Diesel is signposted as "gas oil" pronounced "gas waal"
Petrol is "essence" pronounced "*essongs".*

Gas Oil is a name you may come across elsewhere as well - which will be diesel.

There are many more names - probably as many as there are different countries, but clues like black pumps help, which are usually diesel.

European countries tend to have pumps that are similarly coloured to the U.K. - which may or may not help.

Interestingly at the time of going to print **Hungary** has the lowest diesel price in Europe but if you happen to be touring **Spain,** that advice isn't particularly useful.

Weather:

Best times to visit, depending upon personal preferences.

Eastern Europe: April - October

North Africa: September - March April May

Mid Europe and Turkey: May - October.

Spain, Portugal, Italy, Greece, Southern Europe:

September - May
(Might be rainy during the winter months though)

The U.K. and Ireland:

April - October.

A Scenic Route from Calais in France, travelling east, to Verona in Italy:

Best time to leave: late Spring, Summer or Autumn.

France:

Calais -

Tonnerre:
La Femme de la Fosse Dionne.
A secret well where, since 1758 the locals would carry out laundry duties.
Many metres deep, its source has been a mystery for thousands of years.
Few divers have been able to fathom its depths.

Evian-les-Bains:
Lake Geneva on the **Swiss** border

Chamonix:
Mont Blanc and **Matterhorn** - **Swiss** and **Italian** border.

Italy:

Arona:
Lake Maggiore.
Ferry services and a good sized port.
Breathtaking views.

Como:
If you have had enough driving, the **Car Ferry Terminal**
is at: **Piazza Cavour, Lungo Lario Trieste**.
Ask an Italian local for **'battelli'**.
The Car Ferry operates between the towns of:
Bellagio, Varenna Como, Menaggio and **Cadenabbia**.

Menaggio:
Driving around the left hand side of **Lake Como**
(clockwise).

Sorico:
Great for hiking.
Very peaceful.

Limone Sul Garda:
Picturesque village on the shores of **Lake Garda**.
Great base for sightseeing.

Brenner:
The Brenner Pass.
Well worth taking a drive up the **A22** towards the
Liechtenstein border just for the 'hold onto your
knickers' scenic ride.

Check your brakes are in good working order first!

From Calais to Verona is 24 hours and 1,000 miles - take it very slowly - stop a while to smell and to taste the coffee!!

Descend into **Southern Italy** in an anti clockwise direction:

Note:
San Marino, an independent state, has been included in our guide after the **Italy** section.

Verona:
The two gentlemen of Verona - A Shakespearian comedy written around 1590.
Also the setting for **Romeo and Juliet** (1597).
See a balcony that may, or may not, be the type that Juliet used.
Juliette's House - Hmmm maybe, if you don't mind being squashed in the crowd.
Piazza Delle Erbe - A marvellous open market where you can buy anything.
The Verona Arena - An amazingly well kept **Roman Amphitheatre.**
You can even book tickets to watch events happening here.
The events may, or may not, be gladiatorial.
Torre dei Lamberti - Verona's answer to Blackpool tower but with more panache.

Piazzale Castel San Pietro - Another tower, for the very best views and also, close by, **Teatro Romano,** a **Roman Theatre.**

Don't miss the opportunity to walk over the quaint old bridge - **Ponte Pietra (Peter's Bridge).**

For those of us who plan to see every site in **Verona** it is worth buying a **'Verona Card'** online or at hotels, which allows free entrance to all sites over a period of either 24 or 48 hours for 20 euro or 25 euro.

Bologna:

Well worth booking a walking tour guide initially in order to find your way around.

The first thing that springs to mind when speaking of this wonderful town is **Spaghetti Bolognese**, about which we will say no more.

Here we have so many delicious dishes to sample from. Go to **no. 1 Piazza Maggiore** and enter the vault - **Voltone del Podestà**, and you will discover a wireless telephone that dates back to mediaeval times.

Invented in order to prevent infection from the plague whilst confessing to priests.

The historical porticoes of **Bologna** are well worth looking into from an architectural point of view.

Pescara:

Close to the **Majella National Park.**

Walk or cycle over the **Ponte Del Mare.**

After sunset, when the two branches of the bridge are illuminated, stroll along the riverbanks.

With its red tip and indigo patterns at night, the long, slender spire carrying the structure's cables looks like a space rocket.

When the sun sets, the bridge's two tubes and 161-foot (49-metre) pointed tower will be completely white.

Great clear beaches and fantastic seafood restaurants.

Brindisi:

This is where you may take a car ferry across the **Adriatic** and **Ionian Seas** to **Igoumenitsa** in **Greece**.

Get lost!!!

Sorry not a rude suggestion but enjoy getting lost in the maze of streets and alleyways, sooner or later you will find your way back to the main square.

You can't miss the **Roman Column** erected in the 2nd century.

If you seek out a guided tour you may well be taken to visit the 15th century **Alfonsino castle.**

Not too far away is the **Torre Guaceto nature reserve -** olive groves, marshes and watery creeks.

Calabria:

Aspromonte National Park:
Also **The Valley of the Great Stones.**

A relatively unknown and unexplored wild area in the south of the country.

A wonderful area of forests and mountains, valleys, rivers, lakes, trails and treks.

Here you can find the **Italian Wolf.**

Also rare species of bird such as **Boneli's Eagle** and many other birds of prey.

The whole area is 248 sq miles.

That is a huge area to cover - you may need some time.

The highest peak is **Montalto** at 1,955 metres high.

In the north eastern area you can find **The Queen of the Apromonte** and also **San Luca Pietra Cappa - Pietra Cappa:**

This is the most famous **Monolith** in **Calabria** and the highest in all of Europe..

Reggio Calabria:
Ferry crossing terminal.
Quite a nice beach.

Sicily:

If you would like to visit **Sicily**, in the far south, you must take the ferry across the **Strait of Messina**:

It runs 15 times per week and takes approximately 15 minutes.

The cost is around £15.00.

There are plans to build a suspension bridge from **Reggio Calabria** to **Messina** in **Sicily**.

It will be the longest suspension bridge in the world when, and if, it is ever completed.

It is easily possible to swim across the **Strait of Messina**, in the warm waters of the **Adriatic**.

We have chosen to take a clockwise route around the island of **Sicily**:

We think we've tackled the best sites first by travelling anti clockwise around the island.
If you prefer to leave the best until last then go the other way around.
But that's only a personal view.

Messina:
Ferry crossing terminal.
There is a famous **Astronomical Clock Tower** in the town.

Mount Etna:
An active volcano.
It is well worth hiring a guide once you arrive or even better, book a guided tour from **Catania.**

Taormina:
There is so much to see and do here:
Giardini Naxos.
Mazzarò, Madonna della Rocca Church.
Isola Bella.
But whatever you decide upon, don't miss The **Taormina Greek Theatre.**

Catania:
Mt Etna can easily be seen from here and also a good place to book a personal guided tour.

Visit the busy street markets and the **Cyclops Rocks, Piazza del Duomo** and **Duomo Di Catania.**

Syracuse and the Island of Ortigia:
Excellent for **Archaeological Sites.**
You will need at least two days to search around and still miss a lot.

Noto:
Famous for its **Baroque Architecture.**
Noto Cathedral.

Marzamemi:
Lots of family-run shops and tiny **Art Galleries.**
Great off the beaten track to relax and to eat.

Pozzallo:
Busy port in the south of **Sicily** from where you may board a car ferry to **Malta.**
A fishing port.

Modica:
Visit the **Chocolate Factory.**
The **Cathedral of Saint George.**
Museum of Modica and the **Castello dei Conti.**

Agrigento:
The Valley of the Temples.
Built in the 6th and 5th centuries before Jesus was born.
A must see.

Tickets can be booked online before you visit, to avoid the queues.

Scala dei Turchi:
Stair of the Turks.
Amazingly white bleached rock formations.
Good restaurants.

Palermo:
Although this, one of the best known towns in **Sicily**, is worth a mention, an overnight stay to see the nightlife and bustling city should suffice.

Cefalu:
Very, very popular resort.
Please don't arrive during the summer season.

Will you take another turn around the island of **Sicily** or return across the **Strait of Messina** to mainland **Italy**?

Naples:
'Vedi Napoli e poi muori' - *'See Naples and die'.*
This was a very well used expression describing the esteem that the author, **Johann Wolfgang von Goethe**, had for this town.
It's not as 'touristy' as **Venice** or **Rome**.
Here you will find a multitude of **Art Galleries** and **Architecture** to admire.
A great cultural experience.

The busy port and car ferry terminal is one of the best for both international and local destinations and is teeming with life and activity.

Do not miss the famous sites of **Pompei, Vesuvius** and **Herculaneum.**

Sardinia:

A large island situated off the west coast of **Italy.**

It is in very close proximity to **Corsica.**

Famed for its sun drenched beaches.

There are many ferry routes to **Sardinia** from the west coast, from ports like **Naples, Rome, Pisa** etc. and also from many international ports as well.

For those who like to delve into the past, look out for the hundreds of beehive structures **'Nuraghi'** that date back to the bronze age and are dotted across the island.

Watch out also for the out of this world rock formations.

Rome:

The nation's capital city.

A busy tourist hotspot at most times of the year.

It's often a good idea to get a ticket covering all of the sights in large tourist areas in order to save on buying multiple entry tickets if you plan to visit several.

The Rome Ticket is no exception.

The Colosseum will be near the top of your 'to see' places.

The Column of Marcus Aurelius.

The **Architectural** details of this 2nd century column are well worth seeing.

The Trevi Fountain.

The Pantheon.
The Piazza Navona which was originally an athletics stadium.
The **Underground Catacombs** are a good tour too.

Florence:
A city deep in the heart of **Tuscany** overflowing with **Leather Shops** and **Markets, Museums** and **Galleries, Churches,** and former **Palaces.**
Lots of towers to climb, whether they be in old churches, museums or just for the sake of being a tower.
Pick out your own food in the market and eat like a person who knows how to eat at the **Mercato Centrale.**
Walk along or boat along the famous **River Arno.**
Leave the crowds behind, forget the **Boboli** and walk through the gardens and up the baroque staircase of **Giardino Bardini.**
The **Bardini** has two entrances, one in the **San Niccolò** neighbourhood just past the **Ponte alle Grazie** and the other up on **Costa San Giorgio.**

Pisa:
The Leaning Tower Of
A very busy tourist site.
But if you don't go you will always wonder.
Be prepared for long queues and take a good book with you. Perhaps this one?
There are plenty of expensive restaurants and things to buy.
As with all of the tourist hot spots, watch out for pickpockets.

Padua:

The Taming of the Shrew - A Shakespearian comedy written around 1591 was based in **Padua**.

One of the least visited areas of Italy but arguably one of the best and far cheaper than many more popular towns - like **Venice** for example.

Don't miss a walk along the statue lined canal, for example, you will notice none of the clamour of more well known cities and just as picturesque.

From the square it is a simple task to see some of the city's places of interest, such as the **Santa Justina Basilica**, the **Loggia Amulea** and several **Palaces.**

Venice:

This is another **Italian Port** where a ferry may take you further.

The merchant of Venice - Is a Shakespearian play, written around 1595.

The first call might be **St Mark's Square**.

Watch out for the many street sellers and their wares.

The Marionette Puppets are a particular favourite of mine.

You will enjoy watching the real life **Gondoliers**, (also a **Gilbert and Sullivan Opera)** and marching over **The Rialto Bridge** to experience the amazing **Market** selling many exotic and unusual fish, meat, and virtually everything else besides.

The Bridge of Sighs is another site to watch out for along **The Grand Canal.**

The Bridge was built in 1600 by **Antonie Contino, who** is also, coincidentally, the nephew of the designer of **The Rialto Bridge.**

It was **Lord Byron** who gave the bridge its English name, imagining the last glimpse that the prisoners had as they went over the bridge for interrogation in the **Prison.**

There are many **Art Galleries** and **Museums** here, far too many to mention all, but consider:

The Accademia - This must be the first choice.

Next, **The Peggy Guggenheim Collection.**

You must also visit **The Doge's Palace** and take some boat trips to the Islands around Venice -

Murano - Where you will certainly bring home some glassware.

Burano - To experience the vibrant **Colourful Houses** and to see the amazing **Lace Work.**

Torcello - The first Venetian colony before Venice was colonised.

It was abandoned as a result of plague and malaria.

Trieste:
Grotta Gigante:
This giant cave is the largest in the world.

You will never forget the wonder of this **Gigantic Cave** and surroundings.

Pick a guide who speaks your language. - Fascinating.

San Marino - An Independent State within Italy

A non E.U. member
A non schengen member.
The 5th smallest country in the world.

Blink and you will miss it!

Amazingly, considering the extent to which **Italy** was involved, **San Marino** remained neutral through both world wars.

San Marino is built upon a mountain - **Mt. Titano**.

The town is hilly and cobbled - mainly arranged for tourists, full of expensive gift and souvenir shops, boutiques etc.

Take a walk or a **Tourist Train** up the mountain to visit a **12th century fortress** which has also been utilised as a **Prison** and now houses **Museums** and a **Gallery.**

We suggest that you buy a **Combined Ticket** rather than the **Two Museum Pass.**

The Two Museum Pass allows you to choose two from the following:

Tower 1, Tower 2, St Francis Museum, State Museum, National Gallery of Modern and **Contemporary Art** and **Public Palace.**

A Combined Museum Pass gives entry to **Towers 1 and 2, St Francis Museum, State Museum, National Gallery of Modern and Contemporary Art** and **Public Palace.**

There is also a **Rustic Tourist Train** which will take you on a guided tour and help with the hills.

The Republic of Malta.

An independent Republic

A member of the E.U.
A part of Schengen

Malta is the smallest country in the E.U.

The currency is the Euro.

It is possible to take a vehicle to **Malta** on a car and passenger ferry from the **Sicilian** port of **Pozzallo**.

The journey will take one hour and forty five minutes.

It is impossible to visit Malta without being reminded of **The Knights of St John** who ruled Malta from 1530 to 1798 when **Napoleon** decided to take the country for himself.
Although they did also nearly lose it to **The Ottoman Turks** in 1565.

Places of interest:

Valletta:
A 16th-century citadel and a vibrant 21st-century town. It was built by **The Knights of St John** after they nearly lost Malta to the Ottoman Turks in 1565.
Upper Barrakka Gardens enable panoramic views of **The Grand Harbour.**

The Grandmaster Palace:
Fountain-cooled **Central Square**.
Be prepared for many steps, this is a hilly area.

St John's Co-Cathedral
This is the church of **The Knights of St John** and is
home to two spectacular paintings by **Caravaggio.**
It was built as an 'ordinary church' during 1573 and
1577
For a little piece of 'interesting' information - It is called a
Co-cathedral because it shares the seat of the Roman
Catholic Archdiocese of Malta together with the older
Cathedral of Saint Paul in Mdina.

The Grand Harbour:
Site of the **Great Siege** of 1565 as well as the **Second
World War Encirclement** of 1942.
The harbour lies between **Valletta** and the **Three Cities**.
There are iconic **Castles** on both sides of the water.

Casa Rocca Piccola:
Still home to the **Marquis De Piro** (a modern Knight of
St John) and his family.
Casa Rocca Piccola is a treasure trove of Maltese
antiques and curiosities.
A solid chest, probably the oldest piece of Maltese
furniture in existence, sits alongside intricate Maltese
lace, fascinating family photos, rare paintings and the
only surviving set of silver surgical instruments from the
Knights Sacred Hospital.

Neolithic Temples:
Unesco World Heritage Sites.
The oldest **Stone Architecture** in the world.
Predating both **Stonehenge** and the **Pyramids**.
The temples are proper buildings with monumental doorways, curved rooms, once decorated with plaster and ochre paint, stone furniture and statues.
The originals are now in the **National Museum of Archaeology**.
The best to see are **Mnajdra** and **Hagar Qim**.
Then **Tarxien,** and **Ggantija** on **Gozo**.

St Paul's Catacombs in Rabat.
If you enjoy underground antiquities, you must see **Hal Saflieni Hypogeum:**
A triple-layered **Tomb Complex** of rock-cut chambers.
Different from any in **Rome**.
These catacombs include **Round Stone Tables** where the funerary meal was taken.
Take a torch!!

A Scenic Road Route From Trieste in Italy to Istanbul in Turkey:

Through **Serbia** is the quickest route from **Trieste** in **Italy** to **Istanbul** in **Turkey** by around 700 miles -
1. Slovenia.
2. Croatia.
3. Serbia.
4. Bulgaria.

But the coastal route through **Albania** is far prettier. And you also have the bonus of a trip through **Greece**.

1. Slovenia.
2. Croatia.
3. Montenegro.
4. Albania.
5. Greece.

See the next sections:

Bosnia and Herzegovina:

Is not in the E.U.
Or Schengen.

Safe to visit at the time of going to print but has a reputation for upheaval.

Watch out for landmines outside of the main inhabited areas.

Make sure your passport is stamped on entry.
There are currently no Covid regs.

Old towns and mountains.

More affordable than **Croatia**

Currency:

The Convertible Marka is the unit of currency here. This is subdivided into 100 Pfeninga.
Currently 2.30 Convertible Marka are worth around £1.00.
Approximately 1.8 Convertible Marka are worth 1 U.S. Dollar.
Cash is widely used with transactions often made in Euros and U.S. dollars.

Places of interest:

Mostar - The Stari Most:
The bridge was in existence for 427 years until it was destroyed in 1993.
It has now been rebuilt.

Tuzla Lakes:
Manmade **Salt Lakes.**

Bileca Lake:
A manmade lake.

The Dinaric Alps:
Majestic.
Great for trekking and views.

Sarajevo - The capital city.
Baščaršija:
The old quarter is where you will find many **Market Stalls** and **Bazaars** to explore.
Latin Bridge is the site of the assassination of **Archduke Franz Ferdinand**, which ignited World War I.

Serbia:

Is not quite in the E.U. yet (application in process)
Is not in Schengen.
Therefore British residents can stay for 90 days.
Must register with authorities within 24 hours unless on
a campsite or hotel.

Currency:

The Dinar is the unit of currency here.
Currently 137 Dinar are worth around £ 1.00.
Approximately 107 Dinar are worth 1 U.S. Dollar.

Places of interest:

Belgrade:
Belgrade Fortress.
The River Danube.

Kalemegdan is a massive park housing a **Zoo** and
Museum.
Stroll along the river here and enjoy the views.

Kovin:
Across the river is **Smederevo Fortress.**

The Danube River:
Take a cruise to see the sights along this most famous
river.

Tara National Park:
Take a drive along any of these mountain roads, particularly the 403 for a hair raising 'hold onto your knickers' drive.
Exhilarating.
Tara Park is huge!
One of those, 'not to be missed' adventures.

Resava Cave - Resavska Pecina - A large cave system with many species of bat.

Kosovo:

Is not in the E.U.
Is not in Schengen.
Don't need a visa

Check for current border troubles when travelling.

There are currently border tensions on both the **Serbian** and **Albanian** crossings.

Once inside it is a very safe and secure, friendly country with an exceptionally low crime rate.

Currency:

The Euro is the unit of currency here.
Currently .90 Euro are worth around £ 1.00.
Approximately 1.10 Euro is worth 1 U.S. Dollar.
Most transactions are carried out in cash but there are atm's in the major cities.

Kosovo has some of the most spectacular and beautiful scenery in western Europe.

Places of interest:

Pristina:
The Gracanica Monastery.
There is a cute bear sanctuary here which houses around twenty bears previously kept as pets.

The keeping of bears as pets is now illegal.

Germia Park:
Good for forest treks

Prizren:
Great for traditional architecture and restaurants.

Rugova:
Take a step back into the past.
Absolutely stunning mountainous area filled with picturesque villages, rivers and snow.

Peja:
A shopping town with its own unique local sites and sounds.
Visit **Zenel Beg Tower**.
Try the **Peja Cheeses**!
Here you will also find the **Ethnological Museum**

Bjeshket E Nemuna National Park:
Catch yourself some fish!
An amazing park. You will need several days to explore here.

Gazivoda Lake:
A huge dam on the **Ibar River** shared by **Kosovo** and **Serbia**.

Mirusha Waterfalls:
No less than 12 waterfalls and 13 lakes.

All set within the beauty of a **10 km Canyon.**
You can also see **Caves** here, in the cliffs.
There are some great traditional **Bazaars** to wander
around too.

North Macedonia:

Is not in the E.U.
Or Schengen.
Don't need a visa

Currency:

The Denar is the unit of currency here.
Currently 72 Denar are worth around £ 1.00.
Approximately 56 Denar are worth 1 U.S. Dollar.

Places of interest:

Lots of **Balkan Coffee Shops!**

Skopje:
Capital city. Great nightlife and good base.

Mavrovo National Park:
Bears, lynx, wolves and deer.

Mount Ljuboten:
Lots of wildlife, hawks and eagles.

National park "Galičica":
On the **Albanian** and **Greek** borders to the south of the country.
Excellent lakes, walks, hikes and wildlife.

Slovenia:

See current covid regs.
Is in the E.U.
Is in Schengen

Mountains, ski resorts and lakes.

Currency:

The Euro is the unit of currency here.
Currently .90 Euro are worth around £ 1.00.
Approximately 1.10 Euro is worth 1 U.S. Dollar.

Places of interest:

Ljubljana:
Tivoli Park.
Ljubljana Old Town - Markets and busy streets,
Ljubljana River.

Postojna Cave:
15 miles of **Stalagmites** and **Stalactites.**
A train will wind you through the underground journey.

Skocjan Caves:
Largest caves in the world!
Indescribable. - Amazing!!

Predjama Castle:

A must visit! - a fairy tale, 800 year old castle built into a cave on the side of a mountain… but there's more! Hundreds of tunnels and secret passageways.
Beware you don't get lost!

Triglav National Park South Side:
Tolmin Gorge Trail - A short 2 mile walk through lush canyons, dark tunnels, flowing rivers, and moss-covered rock formations.

Pericnik Waterfall:
A waterfall, or rather two waterfalls, you can walk behind.
View the mountainside from behind a waterfall while you are visiting **Triglav**.
Another don't miss!

Ptuj and Ptuj Castle:
The most charming city of all of eastern Europe - which is a big claim but not unfounded.
Vrsic Pass:
A 'hold on to your knickers' drive over the nation's highest pass.
An epic journey not to be forgotten.

Croatia:

Is in the E.U.
Is in Schengen
Can stay up to 90 days

Accommodation:

Hostel in Split will cost from £ 15.00.
Hotel room in Split will cost from £ 30.00.

Currency:

The Euro is the unit of currency here.
Currently .90 Euro are worth around £ 1.00.
Approximately 1.10 Euro is worth 1 U.S. Dollar.

Places of interest:

Zagreb:
An interesting **Cathedral.**
Several exciting Parks.
A Zoo.
Zagreb is filled with unusual museums.
There is even a museum dedicated to hangovers and one of failed love affairs.
In the **Museum of Illusions** you can find many puzzles, optical illusions and games.
Samobor Castle - Watch out for the very steep incline up to it.

Plitvice - National Park - Lakes and long lazy walks

Krka:
An immense **National Park** filled with rivers, waterfalls, lakes and castles.
The ticket office is on the D56. northside.
There are a few good campsites around this area.
See the **Skradinski Buk Waterfall**.

Split:
The largest city in **Croatia** and along this coast.
It is an interesting **Old Roman town** where many **Roman ruins** remain.
Take a look at **Diocletian's Palace** and **Cellars**.
Klis Fortress and **Bacvice Beach.**

Park Šuma Marjan:
Well worth a drive and stroll around for the views and botanical gardens.
The harbour is a hub of activity and the place for boat and ferry hire.

A week could easily be spent in **Split** exploring.

Hvar:
An island stroll.
The warmest spot on the coast.
Well worth the 1 hour boat ride.
Ferry prices vary depending on times etc.

When travelling south towards **Greece** it is possible to bypass **Bosnia and Herzegovina** by taking the coast road and a right turn at **Komarna,** (you can't miss the brand new **Pelješac bridge**), calling at **Ston** on the peninsula and then returning to the highway D8 near **Zaton Doli**.

Pelješac Peninsula:
Mountains, peaceful villages and warm empty beaches.

Ston:
Mountains, High town walls built up into the mountain, oysters and sea salt.

If you are looking for work here, the salt works take on workers during the summer in summer camps.

Dubrovnik:
Walled town.
Take a boat ride to see some of the many inhabited islands.

Montenegro:

Is not in the E.U.
Or schengen.

Currency:

Despite not being a part of the E.U.
The Euro is the unit of currency here.
Currently .90 Euro is worth around £ 1.00.
Approximately 1.10 Euro is worth 1 U.S. Dollar.

Places of interest:

Durmitor National Park:
Wolves and Bears.
Lots to see - Allow several days.

Author's note:
Durmitor is a bit of a long trek overland from **Dubrovnik**
and could be missed if short of time.
But well worth seeing if not in a rush or coming from a
different direction.

Virpazar - Skadar or **Shkodra Lake**:
The largest lake in southern Europe.
A few days will not be enough for a full exploration.

Albania:

Is not in the E.U.
Or Schengen.
Can stay for 90 days
no visa required
Albania is one of the least dangerous places in Europe.

Currency:

The Lek is the unit of currency here. It is divided into
100 Qindarka but Qindarka are no longer produced.
Currently 130 Leks are worth around £ 1.00.
Approximately 99 Leks are worth 1 U.S. Dollar.

Places of interest:

Tirana:
The capital city.
There are various statues.
The Ring Shopping Centre and **A Museum** dedicated
to its past from the neolithic age through communist
uprisings and to the present day.
The **Grand Park** of **Tirana** is well worth a visit to cool off
and enjoy the massive lake and walks.

Close to **Tirana:**
Divjaka-Karavasta National Park:
Protected coastal lagoons, known for nesting **Dalmatian
Pelicans.**
Boat Rides are also available.

Pogradec:
On the border with **North Macedonia** who share the massive lake.
Taking a ride around the lake involves passing into and through **North Macedonia** but is an excellent spot for a picnic and perhaps a stroll.

Close to **Pogradec:**
Prespa National Park - Parku Kombëtar i Prespës:
On the **Greek** and **North Macedonian** border again.
Excellent National Park filled with wildlife.

Tomorri Mountain National Park - Mount Tomorr:
Skiing and hiking, and canoeing and wildlife.

Vjosë-Nartë Delta:
A Protected Area - **Wetlands** and a **Byzantine Monastery**.

Butrint:
Interesting historical area.
Lots of **Roman Archaeology.**
Visit the **Archaeological Museum.**
The Venetian Triangle Castle.
Eat mussels at **The Mussel House** and relax on **Lori Beach**, from where you can almost touch the **Greek Island** of **Corfu.**
Oh, and if you are up for it, take a peek into one of the many **Bunkers** that are spread around **Albania** - this one is particularly special, being on the **Greek** border.

Qafë-Botë.

If you are a British national travelling from **Albania** to **Greece** you can enter it only by the following land borders:
Kakavia and **Qafë-Botë**. - both in the west.

Travellers must fill in a Passenger Locator Form (PLF) no later than 11:59pm (Greek local time) on the day before arriving in Greece.

Recent update:
It appears that Greece has dropped the requirement to fill in a Passenger Locator Form and have also dropped all covid test requirements.

As always, please keep your eye on any developments.

Romania:

Don't need a visa.

At the time of going to print Romania is a current member of the European Union, however there are some moves for its withdrawal.

The current government is, at present, indifferent to remaining a member, however the general population believe that membership is, and has been beneficial.

Not in Schengen but likely to join in 2023

Shares a border with **Ukraine.**

Passport must be less than ten years old and valid for three months.

Currency:

The Leu is the unit of currency here. It is divided into 100 Bani.
Currently 6 Leu are worth around £ 1.00.
Approximately 4.5 Leu are worth 1 U.S. Dollar.

The food anywhere in Romania is outstanding!!

It is mostly a mountainous Country.

Carpathian Mountains and the Danube Delta.

Places of interest:

Bucharest:
Capital city and by far the largest by some way.
If you are looking for a city experience in Romania this is where you will come to.

It's a good idea to get on a walking tour of the city to give some idea of where you are.
Don't forget to tip at the end.

Salina Slănic Prahova (Mina Unirea):
Salt mine - Both excellent and amazing, vast **Underground Caverns** with viewing platforms and tours.

Transylvania - Bran Castle:
The site of Bram Stoker's fictional Dracula story.

Maramureş:
This is the area for wooden farmhouses, steepled churches and winding roads.
Village life and folk songs - Untouched by tourism - so far.

The Danube Delta:
Boat trips and bird watching or both.
Here you can see the white-tailed eagle, bee-eater, great white egret and the roller.

Moldova:

Is not in the E.U.
Or Schengen.
Don't need a visa
Can stay 90 days.

Sandwiched between **Ukraine** and **Romania.**
With, not quite, a shoreline.

A very poor country but good value for money.
Great for eating out and friendliness..

Has great cultural links with **Romania.**

Lots of vineyards here.

Accommodation:

A night's stay in a hostel can be as little as £ 7.00.
Hotels will start at around £ 30.00. per night.

Currency:

The Leu is the unit of currency here. It is divided into
100 Bani.
Currently 23 Leu are worth around £ 1.00.
Approximately 18 Leu are worth 1 U.S. Dollar.

Forest covered hills and high mountains filled with:

Wild boar, wolves, badgers, wildcats, ermines, martins, and polecats.
Roe deer, hare, foxes, and muskrat.

Europe's least visited country.

Places of interest:

Chișinău:
The capital city.
Cricova winery.
A vast network of caverns used for storing wine.
Wine tasting can be all night, and all day affairs.
There is an **Annual National Wine Festival** here.
Around the capital are no less than 23 lakes.
All good for hiking and views.

Bendery Fortress.

It is difficult to list many interesting sites here without reference to the glorification of the Russian state, which **Moldova** appears to be over keen to do.

Bender - The Transnistrian Train and Railway Museum is interesting in its own way.

Bulgaria:

Is in the E.U.
Not in Schengen - yet, but likely to join in 2023.
Can stay up to 90 days at present.

Food:

Among the most flavorful meat and vegetable dishes are those baked in covered clay pots, such as **kapama** and **kavarma.**

A popular snack and breakfast item is **banitsa,** baked pastry filled with cheese (and sometimes leeks or spinach), washed down by **boza,** a non-alcoholic malted beverage that dates back several centuries.

Currency:

The Lev is the unit of currency here.
Currently 2.3 Lev are worth around £ 1.00.
Approximately 1.8 Lev are worth 1 U.S. Dollar.

Most people pay in cash.

Here, it is normal to nod your head for 'no' and shake your head for 'yes'.

For a 'round the country' tour try our route below:

Places of interest:

Rila Monastery:
One of the largest and also most famous monastery in **Bulgaria** - well worth a visit.
Guided tours are available.

St. Ivan Cave:
The cave where **St. Ivan Rilski** spent seven years of his life.

The Seven Rila Lakes - Glacial lakes.

The above sites can all be visited with a guide on a day tour from Sofia.

https://www.getyourguide.co.uk - local city guides

Sofia:
The capital city lies at the foot of **Vitosha Mountain.**
Excellent for seekers of culture.
Plenty of museums and architecture.
A 4th Century Alexander Nevsky, Roman Cathedral.
Some lush parks.
Boyana Waterfall is good for views and a hike.

Lovech:
Smashing town, Not far from **Sofia**.
Some fascinating sites.
See the **Covered Bridge** over the **River Osam**.
There is also a **Mediaeval Fortress** and the **Vasil Levski Museum**.

Devetaki - Devetàshka Cave:
Take the path by the river.
The site has been continuously occupied by Paleo humans for tens of thousands of years,

Krushuna Falls:
Take good walking shoes and water.
The cost is 5 Lev, don't forget to take a map from the man and choose the **Red Route.**
One of the best waterfalls in the land.

The above sites too can all be visited with a guide on a day tour from **Sofia**.

Varna:
Sea port and seaside resort.
Famous for **The 'Gold of Varna'** - A 6,000 year old **Thracian Jewel** which is held in **The Archaeological Museum** along with many other Greek, Roman and Ottoman treasures.
There is also a **Grand Promenade** and **Primorski Park**.

Plovdiv:
Once named **Philippopolis**.
If you are looking for **Roman Amphitheatres** forget **Rome,** all of **Italy** and **Greece.**
Plovdiv has the world's best preserved **Ancient Theatre**.
It is still in use today.

Also - **The Maritsa River** and **Tsar Simeon Park**.
For a stroll and scenic beauty.

Greece:

Is in the E.U.
Is In Schengen.

Driving in Greece, the vehicle entering a roundabout has priority, and if you are going around the round-about, you have to give way.

Another useful tip is that most people driving where you are driving won't be Greek and therefore probably won't be aware of this.

Greece is popular, not only for the abundance of historical sites, but also for its long summer sunshine.

There are very many beautiful and interesting islands off the coast that reach as far as the **Turkish** coastline.

These are widely the destinations organised by travel agents and are the most popular.

There are car and passenger ferries which regularly transport to many of these beautiful islands.

The major ports:

Piraeus, Santorini, Mykonos.
The capital city, **Athens,** has three main ports, **Piraeus, Rafina and Lavrion.**
Thessaloniki is also an option - there are others.

It would be as well to book ferry tickets well in advance, before your trip as they are unlikely to be available at short notice.

Although many islands have ferry ports, they are not all interconnected and it may not be possible to reach another island from the one you are visiting.

For an in depth guide to **Greek ferries,** check out:

https://www.davestravelpages.com/ferries-in-greece/

Currency:

The Euro is the unit of currency here.
Currently .90 Euro are worth around £ 1.00.
Approximately 1.10 Euro is worth 1 U.S. Dollar.

Places of interest:

Igoumenitsa:
A harbour town.
The place to disembark, or embark, from a ferry going to, or from, **Brindisi** and **Venice** in **Italy**.

Missolonghi:
Salt Museum.
Was once owned by the **Venetians.**
Famous for **The 'Three Sieges of Missolonghi'**.
Lord Byron died here.

Rion-Antirrion Bridge - Fantastical suspension bridge.

Patras:
The Patras Carnival is not only the biggest carnival in Greece, it is also one of the biggest and best carnival celebrations in all of Europe.
It always begins on the 17th January and lasts for ten days.

Corinth:
The Isthmus of Corinth.
Well worth investigating its history.
7,000 year old town.

Mycenae:
The site of the city of **King Agamemnon** who led the battle against Troy during the Trojan war as related by **Homer.**

Epidaurus:
A Greek Amphitheatre built 332 - 320 years before Jesus was born.
Is still in use today.

Athens:
The apocalypse, (as my wife refers to it).
The Acropolis.
Roman Temple.
The Parthenon.
Watch out for pickpockets.

Athens is known for being the birthplace of democracy. The Greeks have a lot to answer for.

Delphi:
Phocis:
Breathtaking landscapes.
Sitting on **Mount Parnassus** with great views of the **Gulf of Corinth**.
Once considered by the Ancient Greeks to be the centre of the world.
Delphi is also home of **The Sanctuary of Apollo.**

Trikala:
Meteora is a high rock formation upon which six, there were originally 24, monasteries are built.
Quite a spectacle visually and geologically unique.
All of these monasteries can be visited - a tour guide who speaks your own language is useful.

Mount Olympus:
Mytikas Peak.
Home of the fictional Greek gods.

Thessaloniki:
A port city on **The Thermaic Gulf**.
Very much cheaper than **Athens**.
English is widely spoken.
Good for foodies.
Many places to eat with friendly locals.
Accommodation here is much cheaper too.
Great beaches.

Paul suffered some severe persecution here, as did the community that subsequently thrived after his departure. Paul, with Timothy and Barnabus, laid a good foundation of God's kingdom which stood the young believers in good stead despite the false teachers who attempted to lead them astray.
Sadly, some two thousand years later, that foundation is in need of some reinforcement.

Greek islands:

There are approximately 6,000 islands off the mainland of Greece.
227 0f them are inhabited.

Some of which are ridiculously close to the **Turkish** coast.
We will not attempt to list them all here.

Feel free to send us your favourite places and we will be delighted to add a review under your name if you wish.

Go here for one of the better and most inclusive island guides and how to reach them:

https://www.davestravelpages.com/ferries-in-greece/

Crete:
Beaches, mountains, gorges, monasteries, caves and villages.
The ferry from **Piraeus**, will take approx 6 hours.

A moped is a good, cheap way to get around here. You will need at least five days to explore **Crete** properly.

Knossos:

Once the centre of the mighty **Minoan** civilisation. Famous for the **Minotaur** of Greek legend. With the body of a man and the head of a bull, supposed to live in a vast underground labyrinth. Don't miss the **Knossos Palace.**

The Samaria Gorge:

An excellent hike, well worth the effort.

Chania:

16th century lighthouse and interesting, nay, charming town.

The Archaeological Museum of Heraklion:

Among the most important museums in **Greece**. Its exhibits include representative samples of all the historical and prehistoric periods of **Crete**, covering a period of 5,500 years from the Neolithic till the Roman times.

It also hosts the masterpieces of the Minoan civilization and exhibits findings from **Knossos**, **Phaestos**, **Zakros**, **Malia** and other important Minoan excavations on the island of **Crete.**

Frangokastello Castle and beach.

Vai Beach is where an advert for the **Bounty Chocolate Bar** was once filmed.

Spinalonga island - once a leper colony.

Naxos:
The ferry from **Rafina** will take approximately 5 hours.

Santorini:
The very best island for a honeymoon.
The ferry from **Lavrio** will take approximately 8 - 9 hours but also stops at **Kea, Kythnos, Serifos and Folegandros.**

Each one of which is another 'must not miss' adventure.

Santorini is smaller than other islands and easy to find a different beach to chill on every day.
It is one of the most expensive Greek islands so be aware.
It is also one of the most popular tourist destinations in Europe.
There is an **Active Volcano.**

Kea:
Loulis, - **Kea's capital town**.
The Monastery of **Panagia Kastriani.**
Ancient Karthea 6th Century Monument - Great hiking.
A shorter 3 km walk can be taken from the village of **Chavouna**.
The Ancient Lion Landmark - Another great walk.
Akrotiri Kefalas and **Agia Arini -** Neolithic settlements in the north of the island..

Kythnos:
Very pretty villages with a population of just 1800.
Lots of quiet beaches, walking and peace.
Loutra - Healing hot springs

Serifos:
Quite a busy, popular island.
According to the myth:
Perseus arrived at the shores of Serifos with his mother,
Danae, locked in a chest.
To punish Polydectes, King of Serifos, he killed the
Gorgon Medusa [a mythical creature] and showed him
her severed head: upon seeing it, Polydectes turned to
stone.
Mining Sites and lots of beaches.
Koutalas - Seaside village with beautiful natural
surroundings and beaches.
Kastro tis Grias - meaning - **Old Lady's Castle -** on
the hill, overlooking **Koutalas** and the **Cave** where you'll
see stalactites and stalagmites in really odd shapes.
Chora - A short walk up steps to the **Castle.**
Livadi - A most picturesque harbour well worth seeing.

Folegandros - Built upon high cliffs, quite magnificent!
An untouched island and very beautiful.
Chora - (a popular village name in Greece) - a picture
postcard village, visit **The Venetian Quarter.**

Mykonos - Popular for nightlife and clubbing.
The windmills are interesting.
The ferry trip takes 4 hours from **Piraeus**

Kos:
In the northeast of Kos - The Asclepion Temple.
Established in the 2nd and 3rd century b.c.
From here you can see the Turkish coast line.
Very close by but built approximately six hundred years
later **- Casa Romana.**
Slightly older - **The Roman Odeon of Kos**
Neratzia Castle - Built in the middle ages **A Knight's
Templar Castle** - A castle-fortress enclosing an entire
settlement.
Antimachia Castle - Quite close to **Kos airport,** It
controlled the passage between the islands of **Kos** and
Nisyros.
Kos has very many interesting ancient monuments.
An island guide would be a great help in touring here.

Corfu:
The ferry to **Corfu** from **Igoumenitsa** takes
approximately two hours.
The Imperial Palace of Achillion - the summer retreat
of **Empress Elisabeth of Austria** is just a short drive
away from **Corfu** Town.
The Mon Repos Palace and the **New and Old Corfu
Fortress** are worth visiting too.
Kontokali is the village where the famed **Durrell family**
once lived.
Kalami Bay - where **Lawrence Durrell (Larry)** once
lived with his wife

Dodecanese Islands:
Now owned by Greece.

Rhodes is the capital of these.
There are 15 large islands in this group and 150 smaller ones.
Only 26 of these are inhabited.

Strangely it was the **Italians** who made many improvements and restorations on these islands but the locals' preference was for **Greek** rule.

Turkey does not appear to be interested at all, mainly because the inhabitants have always been **Greek**.

Rhodes:
The largest of the **Dodecanese Islands**
Tucked under the south west tip of **Turkey**.
The ferry from **Piraeus** will take approximately 20 hours and from **Crete** 14 hours.
Visit **The Acropolis of Lindos.**
The Valley of Butterflies.
The Monastery of Filerimos.
Shopping, Eating, Beaching and Watersports figure strongly on **Rhodes** but also a great base to go **Island Hopping** from.

Patmos:
It takes a little over 11 hours to travel on a ferry from **Piraeus** to **Patmos**.

There are around 3000 people who live permanently on the Island.

Great Beaches and lots of sunshine.

The Romans used **Patmos** in a similar way that the British government once used Australia - as a place to send those who caused problems.

Famous for being the island where John was exiled to and had the revelation and experience of meeting Jesus.

It was during that meeting that Jesus warned of the need to change, to renew our love for Him and each other.

Jesus explained how His kingdom would be established on earth, when that change would come about and how His people will be filled with Him on earth - A change that is now occurring.

It was whilst John was on **Patmos** that Jesus warned of the fate of 'Babylon' - the worlds, political, economical and religious systems - all that is not built upon Spirit.

When Jesus was on earth He also taught that there would be many who believed they were His children but in truth, don't know Him.

In John's vision Jesus offered many 'crowns' or rewards for those who He knew and had faith in him.

One of the rewards is to reign with Him on earth.

The extent to which we are able to achieve the prizes that are offered is dependent upon how we respond to Him whilst we live.

Are our lives filled with faith?
Do we trust Him for our everyday needs?
Are we 'overcoming' the enemy who wants to pull us down and restrict the growth of God's Kingdom?

Do we have faith that what Jesus achieved for us in His life, death and resurrection is sufficient to bring us into a loving relationship with Him?

Do we know Him?
Is He relevant in our lives?
Or do we simply please ourselves?

How our faith in Him is reflected in our lives today will be a deciding factor of our lives into eternity.

The Revelation: All of which was given to John whilst he was in exile, living on **Patmos.**

More Greek Islands:

There are over 6000 **Greek Islands** to explore.
Many are uninhabited.
The challenge is to find and enjoy those less frequented.

The Presidential Republic of Cyprus:

Geographically in Asia but culturally and politically still within Europe.

Is in the European community but not in Schengen.

The inhabitants are half Turkish and half Greek.
The line of division in the country was abolished in 2004.

Driving is on the left hand side.

Currency:

The Euro is the currency here.

Places of interest:

Paul, Barnaby and Mark visited Cyprus.
They walked from **Salamis**, in the east, to **Pathos**, in the west, some 90 miles.
Approximately the same distance as it would be to walk from Birmingham to London.

Troodos Mountains - good for hiking

Protaras - Fig tree bay

Nicosia - Cyprus Museum and **City Walls**

Limassol Castle.

Paphos - beaches and archaeological sites.

Europe Meets Asia:

Turkey:

90 days in 180 days maximum stay allowed.
Consecutively or at different times.

Is not in the E.U.
Is not in Schengen.

Turkey is where Eastern Europe meets Western Asia.

Driving:

There are many toll roads in Turkey.
It is essential, or at least, sensible, that you obtain an **HGS** sticker to go on your windscreen to avoid fines.
This negates the need to stop at toll booths.
The HGS sticker can be loaded with credit from petrol stations, Turkish post offices and some banks.
It can also easily be recharged on the internet. - pttbank.ptt.gov.tr

Vehicle rental is around £30.00. per day in Turkey.

Hotel costs are around £20.00 Per night for a 2 star and £35.00 per night for a 4 star.

When to be in Turkey:

March and December are the cheapest months.
June is the Apricot season in **Malatya**
Late October - November is the **Saffron Festival** in **Safranbolu**
The Cappadocian Balloon Festival is at the end of August.

Weather:

South is okay from late April to October.
Best not travel in the northeast during winter months.
It can be very cold and the mountain roads are treacherous.

From **Van** in the east, to **Istanbul** in the west, is 20 hours travel time by car.

Before you leave home, and whilst travelling, read any book by **Yaşar Kemal**:
Memed my hawk.
They burn the thistles.
Iron earth, copper sky.
The wind from the plain.
The birds have also gone.
There are many others.

Dining:

Mücver - traditional fried meatballs prepared with chopped zucchini.

Try **menemen** for breakfast - A sort of soup made from eggs, tomatoes and onions.
Or **Turkish Pancakes**! - **Gozlem** - Yummy.

To drink with that? - **Şalgam** - red turnip juice.
You won't need to eat another meal for a long time.

Unless, of course, you come across **'icli pide'** - stuffed with mincemeat - delicious.
Once tasted you will never want to go back to pizza again.

Pide ekmegi is a very tasty flatbread, eaten on its own or with any meal.

Pide is the predecessor to pizza.

Garnished pide is known by many names depending upon the topping or region:

Kasarli pide - with cheese.
Kasarli-yumurtali pide - with cheese and eggs.
Kavurmali pide, - 'roasted', which can be garnished with different ingredients. This is crunchy.
Kiymali pide - with mincemeat.
Ispanakli pide - with spinach.
Kusbasi etli pide - with diced beef.
Pastirmali-yumurtali - with pastrami and eggs.
Sujuk pide - Turkish sausage.
Peynirli pide - with cheese.
Sarimsakli pide - with garlic.

Tahinli pide - with tahini.
Karadeniz pide - from the black sea.
All pide from the black sea areas are called **kastamonu kir pidesi** which means of the grasslands - very similar to **lahmacun.**

And now you know all there is to know about **pide!**

Also, try **Kumpir** - the best stuffed potato ever.

Currency:

The Lira is the unit of currency here.
It is divided into 100 kuruş.
Currently 30 Lira are worth around £ 1.00.
Approximately 24 Lira are worth 1 U.S. Dollar.

Places of interest:

Ankara:
Turkey's capital city.
Situated on a hill.
Ancient Fort - **Roman Baths** and lots more.
Once named **Angora.**
Famous for its **Angora Wool**, white rabbits, and Angora cat.
Gençlik Park - Attend The Night Pool Show.
Eat yoghurt.
Atakule - See the heights from way up high.

North Black Sea Coast:

Sinop:
Harbour - parks - nature reserve.

Sinop to Trabzon - 7 hours.
Sinop to Ankara to Kulu to lake Tuz - 7 hours

North Western Turkey:

Safranbolu:
A hilly town.
An out of the way spot to visit.
Its name comes from the Saffron plant.
Visit the **Annual Saffron Festival** in late October -
November.
Be sure to see the **Carsi District.**
There is an excellent **Market** and **Bazaar.**
Cinci Han Caravansary - Is a mediaeval inn.
Several very interesting museums.

Istanbul:
Hagia Sophia.
Topkapi Palace.
Taksim Square.
The Grand Bazaar.
Here you can buy anything.
A wonderful atmosphere and very friendly stall holders.
Rumeli Hisari - Rumeli Fortress.
An amazing fortress, built in the Ottoman era.
Well preserved and a good size.

You will need a good day here.
Great museum alongside too.

Eminönü - This is Istanbul at its best - A fantastic harbourside experience with the hustle and bustle of busy market stalls and restaurants. Fish delicacies and sea views.

To the north of **Istanbul** there are at least eight amazing parks to visit.

Belgrad Forest is a huge wooded area - great for **Hiking.**
At the heart of **Belgrad Forest** is **Büyük Dam.**

To the east, on the **Asian** side of **Istanbul,** is **Ömerli Barajı Kam -** An immense area of beautiful woodlands surrounding a massive dam.
There are plenty of good camping sites and wild camping available all around the dam.

Travelling South from Istanbul:

West coast:

On the **Aegean sea:**

Bursar:
Silk markets and parks -
Taste a delicious **Iskender Kebab**

Bergama:
The ancient Greek town of **Pergamon** or **Pergamum.**
Sits proudly on a hill.
It is likely that it was Paul's teaching that founded a church here.
John was told to write a letter to the community warning them of the false teaching that 'the church' still teaches today.
There is an interesting **Roman Theatre** here.

Izmir/Smyrna:

The seven communities addressed by John are all within this area:
Ephesus, Smyrna, Pergamum, Thyatira, Sardis, Philadelphia and **Laodicea.**
There are some very fascinating archaeological remains.

Selcuk:
Ancient **Ephesus - Temple of Artemis of the Greeks** and **Diana of the Romans.**
Look out for the **Market Square** where Paul, Priscilla & Aquila worked as tent makers.
Paul had a tough relationship with the Ephesians.
John also wrote to the Ephesian community from **Patmos -** now a Greek island in the Adriatic sea.
Selcuk, or Ephesus, as it was then, is the town where Mary and John lived with the community of Christians there.

Pamukkale:
Very close to the ancient city of **Laodicea**.
White cliffs - mineral-rich thermal waters flowing down white travertine terraces on a nearby hillside - Very picturesque, even now.

Hierapolis - **Archaeology Museum** and **Ancient Greek Amphitheatre.**

The Mediterranean Sea:

Bodrum:
Bodrum Castle.
From here cruise to **Fethiye** and then cruise back again to **Bodrum** with the **Blue Cruises.**
Crystal clear turquoise water and fish!

Hisarönü:
Here you might join **The Lycian Way** for a hike.
It is **520 km** in length and stretches from **Hisarönü,** to **Aşağıkaraman** in **Konyaaltı.**
A good three day stroll.

Marmaris:
Harbour - enjoy a delicious fish sandwich on the harbour walls.
Follow in the footsteps of **Yaşar Kemal** the Turkish author.

Dalyan:
On the **Dalyan River.**

Absolutely beautiful area - Stunning!

Sultaniye:
On the shore of **Lake Köyceğiz**:
Here there are **Thermal Mud Baths.**
It is an absolute must to drive around the lake at least once.
Take the riverboat connection to **Iztuzu Beach** where the protected **Loggerhead Turtle** nest.

Kaunos/Caunos:
Across the river from **Dalyan** there are the **Lycian Rock Tombs, Tombs of the Kings** and the remains of a **Theatre**.

Fethiye:
Turquoise water.
Butterfly Valley Nature Reserve.

Oludeniz:
Blue Lagoon - White beaches.

Patara - Beach and ruins.

Kas:
Southernmost point - Rock tombs - White washed houses.

Kemer:
Mount Olympus Nature Park.
Mount Tahtali - **Mount Olympus.**

This is the highest mountain in **Kemer** - 2365 metres.
There is a cable car that will take you to the top.

Antalya:
An **Ancient Roman Port** now a fantastic **Harbour** filled with all sorts of harbour life.
Don't miss the triumphal three arches known as
Hadrian's Gate.
Duden Waterfalls are worth seeing, around 15 minutes drive east from the main town.

Sagalossus:
An ancient archaeological site excavating a temple and surrounds dedicated to the Roman Emperor Hadrian.
This is clearly an area where a Hadrian cult worshipped

Aspendos:
Aqueduct.
Bridge.
And a **Greek Theatre**.

Alanya:
Cleopatra's Beach.
Alanya Castle.

Tarsus:
Paul's home town.
Jewish citizens of **Tarsus** were granted Roman citizenship, which is why Paul's scourging with whips and imprisonment were unlawful and why he was able to appeal to Caesar.

Adana:
Riverside parks, mosques, and traditional bazaars,
where tiny restaurants serve the local speciality:
Try an **Adana Kebab** - speciality.

From Adana to Sanilurfa is only 4 hours.

Gaziantep: Good for food restaurants.
For breakfast, or anytime really, ask for **'beyran
çorbası'** - A type of lamb soup with rice, garlic and
pepper paste. Add a dash of **pul biber** or **acili** for extra
oomph!

South Eastern Turkey:

***Harran -** Amazing ancient ruins - fascinating. Abram
lived here for a while.

***Balıklı Göl Cd**. - Abrams pool

***Şanlıurfa - Urfa museum**. (pronounced *'shan-ler-fa')*

***Gobekli Tepe - Potbelly hill** - 12,000 years old.

***Karahan Tepe -** a recently discovered ancient
community, a sister site to **Gobekli Tepe** which was
inhabited - a mere 600 years earlier.

*__All within one hour's travel.__

Continue east to **Kortik Tepe -** 12,400 - 11,700 years old and then on to **Lake Van** or travel north?

On the Euphrates River:

From Harran Travelling North:

4 hours to

Mount Nemrut - **Nemrut Dağı Yolu:**
Beautiful scenery.
An Ancient Royal Tomb.
Head Statues.

Malatya:
The world's leading **Apricot** producer - look out for the **Apricot Bazaar** - June is the month to be here.
This is quite a wealthy town for this area.
Must visit - **Turgut Özal Nature Park.**
Battalgazi - Take a tour guide (possibly in a minibus) from **Malatya** to the restored **Silahtar Mustafa Pasha Caravanserai.**
Günpınar Waterfall.
Malatya Castle.
For bazaars go to:
Esnaflar Bazaar.
Sire Bazaar and
Bakircilar Bazaar.

Keban Dam - Immense Dam.
Fascinating!

Elazig:
Harput Castle.
Keban Barrage - another dam.
Palu Kalesi - Palu Castle.
Dabakhane - Hot springs and geysers.

From Elazig to Tatvan (Van) is about 7 hours.

Suggest that you go to **Mount Ararat** and **Van** after **Cidir Lake**.

North Eastern Turkey: - Warm Months Only.

Travelling North:

Erzurum: - Authors note: (Could be missed)?

Erzurum has always been a centre for trading, a crossroads.
One of the wealthier towns in this area but small enough to walk around quite quickly.
Go to the **Castle**.
Erzurum Kalesi:
The minaret is worth the climb in order to see the city but it may be closed and there isn't much else to see here.

Erzincan may be - **Is definitely,** a better stop off between **Elazag** and **Karaca Mağarasi** than **Erzurum**.

Erzincan:
Otlukbeli Golu - take a tour guide with you.

Girlevik Waterfall:
Breathless beauty but try to pick a less busy time to go.

Kemaliye Karanllk Kanyon - See the **Mountain Goats!!**
Take a boat as well for an extra special day out.

Karaca Mağarası - Karaca Cave.
Timeless and unmissable.

Soumela Monastery - Epic!

Anatolian Steppe - Grassy plains and mountainous peaks.

Trabzon:
On the Black sea coast.
Good to stay here for several days.
Maybe use it as a base to tour from?
Has long been plagued by **Pirates** from all eras and cultures.
Famous for its anchovies called **Hamsi.**
Try also:
Beet - made with black cabbage.
Laz pastry.
Akcaabat Meatballs.
Grey Mullet Sour.

Golia.
The staff in the tourist office speak very good english.
Taş Han. A former **Caravanserai** - Restored
The **City Walls** are fascinating to walk around and can be viewed from **Zagnos Bridge and Park.**
Far too many **Parks** to mention and all of them very peaceful and worth visiting.

Uzungöl:
A Lake in the mountains with a very old village.

Anzer Yaylasi:
More beautiful than anything you know or can imagine!!!

Rize - Ayder Plateau:
Gorgeous - Waterfalls.
The **Laz & Hemsin Communities** are very welcoming and friendly.

Palovit Waterfall:
The biggest waterfall in the Black sea region.
The views from the road leading up to it is worth the trip on its own.
Quite cold in winter and some roads are impassable.
Visit in summer only.

Zilkale:
The greatest Castle in Turkey's **Rize Province**.
Firtina Valley - Beautiful.
To eat - **Mıhlama (or Muhlama)**

Kackar Mountains:

Borcka Karagol Nature Park:

Artvin:
Waterfalls - Nature Reserves.

Karagöl Altıparmak - A must see!!!

Çıldır Lake:
Stunning! - Incredibly beautiful - The best place to go around **Kars** - Breathtaking scenery.

Kars:
High on a plateau overlooking a valley and river.

From Kars to Mount Ararat is about 3 hours

Ani - Ani Ocakli - Large area.
An abandoned **Armenian Village**.
Some **Caves** - On a plateau.
Can't be missed but a guide may be useful.
This has historically been a disputed area but access appears to be ok from the **Turkish** side at present.

See Places of interest in **Armenia.**

Eastern Turkey:

Keep well away from the **Iranian** border.

Agri Dagri:
Mount Ararat:
The mountain that **Noah's Ark** rested upon.

Tatvan:
Lake Van - Beautiful.
Nemrut Crater Lake - Famous for swimming cats.

From **Van** to **Kayseri**:

Kortik Tepe:
A must see **Archaeological Dig** which is 12,400 - 11,700 years old.

Mid Turkey:

Cappadocia:

Kayseri:
A very interesting area.
Try to eat - **Kayseri Mantısı** - Mince meat in dough balls
Drink - **Gilaburu juice.**

Belisirma:
Cute little stone houses scattered to the slopes of **Ihlara Valley.**
Amazingly fantastical **Cave System.**
Drive via **Nevsehir**, **Acigol** and **Gulagac**.
See:
https://www.turkeytourorganizer.com/blog/belisirma-village

Nevşehir Merkez/Nevşehir:
Be sure not to miss the spectacular **Hot Air Balloon Festival** at the end of August.

Yay Golu - Saline pink salt lake

Goreme Historical National Park:

Soganli Valley - Rock cut buildings

Pasabag Valley - also known as **Monks Valley:**
Fairy chimneys and cone shaped rocks.
Valley of the Monks is a must see!!

Uchisar Castle - Amazing - another must visit!

Rose Valley:
Visit here at sunset to get the best colours.
The volcanic rock formations are known as **Fairy Chimneys.**
They were formed thousands of years ago.
Some were once inhabited.
Visit also - **Crusader Church, Column Church.**

Zemi Valley:
Zemi Valley is one of the best hidden gems in Cappadocia.
The valley is situated just outside of Goreme, making it the perfect place to visit on foot.

Most people come to **Zemi Valley** to hike its short loop, which only takes about an hour.
Along the way, there are some pretty impressive and massive **Fairy Chimneys** to be seen, especially the ones in the **Gorkundere Valley.**

The **Zemi Valley** connects to the **Goreme Sunset Viewpoint,** which is an excellent and easy spot to get to from Goreme.
But going from the town requires you to pay a small entrance fee, going from **Zemi Valley is free.**

The Three Zelve Valleys:
The best museums in the region – **The Zelve Open-Air Museum.**
Unlike the **Goreme Open-Air Museum** which has a huge collection of rock-carved churches, the **Zelve Open-Air Museum** was a settlement inhabited by people until 1952.

Imagination Valley - or **Devrent Valley.**
Cool Fairy Chimneys and Camels!

Near **Kulu - Lake Tuz:**
Pink salt lake famous for flamingos but disappearing through drought

Konya - **Çatalhöyük**:
A large neolithic site - neolithic houses.

Georgia:

Is not in the E.U.
Or schengen.
Nice place to visit.

Do not need a visa
U.K.residents can stay without a visa for up to one year!
Unless working.
If that period is exceeded a fine will be given on exit.

A U.K. resident can drive for up to one year on a U.K.
driving licence.
After that period it is necessary to have an International
driving licence.

Relatively safe with a low crime rate.

Accommodation:

It is easily possible to rent some rooms across the
country for around £150.00. Per month.
A hotel room can cost from £ 30.00.per night.

Currency:

The **Lari** is the unit of currency here. It is divided into
100 **Tetri.**
Prices are often advertised in euros and dollars as well
but should be paid for in Lari.
Currently 3.5 Lari are worth around £1.00.

Approximately 2.5 Lari are worth 1 U.S. Dollar.

Food:

Before we go any further, in **Georgia**, joining a **Supra Feast** is essential!

Most cities will organise a **Supra** for tourists to enjoy - ask at a local tourist office or even a hotel.

But the most authentic way to enjoy a **Supra** is to become friendly with a local family.

Also, sample - **Lobio** and baked mushrooms filled with **Sulguni** (local) cheese.
Lobio is a bean soup that's cooked in a clay pot with herbs and spices and served with fresh coriander.

You can't visit Georgia without tasting **Khachapuri - Georgian cheese bread.**

We have used **Tbilisi** as a centre for our routes spreading out in either the north, south, east or westerly directions.

Places of interest:

Tbilisi:
The capital city.
The old town is remarkable .
Lots of **Theatres** and **Museums**.

Book a tour of **Ani Ocakli** from here.

Narikala Fortress:
More of a skeleton than a fortress these days as it was blown up by a Russian munitions explosion in 1827. Nevertheless there are very picturesque ruins.
Take a ride on the massive **Cable car/aerial tramway.**

Mtskheta:
World Heritage Site.
Old village.
Lots of religious sites.
Monasteries

Caves of Uplistsikhe:
Inhabited since the early 2nd century before Jesus.
A complex village carved out of rock.

Borjomi:
Famous for its mineral water.
Borjomi Central Park - Free entrance if you stay at a local hotel.
Borjomi National Park - Virgin forests where there are bear, lynx, wolf, red deer and chamois.

Chiatura:
Manganese Mines.
Rusty cable cars and amazing scenery.

Vardzia:
A **Cave Monastery** site on the **Kura River**.

Kutaisi:
Said to be one of the oldest inhabited cities in the world.
Lots of scrummy places to eat.
Visit the market.
Swim in the **Tskaltsitela River** near **Solomon Meore Street.**
Zarati Waterfall.
Motsameta Monastery.
Gelati Monastery.
Colchis Fountain.
Bagrati Cathedral.
Sataplia Nature Reserve.
Kutaisi Botanical Gardens.

Bakhmaro:
High mountain resort with no water supply and often no electricity supply.

Batumi:
On the **Black Sea** coast.
Beach - no sand, just pebbles.
Botanical gardens by the sea.
130 metre high **Alphabetic Tower** with observation deck.

Lake Ritsa:
A lake in the **Mountains** of **Abkhazia.**
The area is known as the **Ritsa Relict National Park.**
There are boat rides on the lake and a bazaar, as well as authentic restaurants.

Svaneti:

A Medieval Land.

The province of **Svaneti** is dotted with hundreds of ancient **Watchtowers** which for years helped the locals keep invaders at bay.

Eat - **Khachapuri** - It's a bit like cheese bread - various flavours.

Racha-Lechkhumi Svaneti National Park

Ushguli and other villages are worth touring around for their uniqueness.

Ananuri:

90 mins north of **Tbilisi** - Two churches joined by a wall overlooking the river - Stunning.

Fortress Complex. Great for historical dialogue.

Kazbegi - **National Park:**

Stunning. Spellbinding, absolutely magnificent!

Mkinvartsveri.

Kazbegi Mountains:

In the **Caucasus Region**.

Mountainous region with snow capped peaks.

Valleys and canyons.

Very beautiful but busy and dangerous road.

On the Russian border.

Many heavy Russian trucks queue here to get over the border.

There is a new road and tunnel being built which may make life easier for traffic.

Kakheti:
Monastery and **Caves of Gareji,** approximately two hours from **Tbilisi.**
It is well worth the journey.
There are 70 caves, 2 temples, one fortress, a sacred place and tons of other buildings in this complex.
A word of warning, it is on the disputed **Azerbaijan** border and the source of much conflict.

Sighnaghi:
One of the prettiest towns in this area.
City walls and fortifications.
Some great places to eat local food.
This is a wine making region so lots of opportunities to taste great wines too!

Tusheti:
Tusheti National Park.
Very dusty and dangerous road.
Good for the adrenaline!!

Omalo and other local villages.
A rural area three hours from **Tbilisi.**

The Obano Pass:
More of a dust track than a road.
Featured as being the world's most dangerous road.
Several deaths here every year.

Watch out for the **wild ponies** that roam here.

Very isolated area.

Cut off from the world for most of the year and only accessible during the summer months when it is very hot.

Stay in one of the little wooden houses or just camp in the mountains.

Well worth reading the following article by **Nadia Beard** in the **Guardian Newspaper,** before arriving, in order to give some perspective and understanding of the area.

https://www.theguardian.com/travel/2021/nov/26/tourism -rescues-omalo-georgia-from-oblivion-photo-essay

Armenia:

No visa required.

Can stay up to six months.

Not part of the E.U. but very friendly.

Armenia was one of the first nations to declare itself a Christian country in 301 A.D.

As of 2011 some 90% of Armenians will still claim Christianity as their national religion.
Whether that claim is simply a religious stance or one of real life is debatable.

Currency:

The **Dram** is the unit of currency here. It is divided into 100 **luma** and is also used in the neighbouring unrecognised Republic of Artsakh.
Currently 500 Dram are worth around £1.00.
Approximately 400 Dram are worth 1 U.S. Dollar.

Places of interest:

Yerevan:
The **Capital City** of **Azerbaijan.**
Sitting alongside **The Hrazdan River.**
Known as the city of cafes.

Plenty of opportunity for exercise here in one of the city's many parks.

The Grand Republic Square is interesting as is climbing **The Cascade** to see the **Monument** to the city's Soviet past.

There is an **Opera Theatre** and several **Museums.**

There is even a **Zoo.**

Visit the **Blue Mosque.**

The Armenian Genocide Memorial is an eye opener.

Arinj - 20 minutes drive from **Yerevan.**

Levons Divine Underground Structure is unlike anything conceived before.

A labyrinth of caves 7 floors deep.

Totally man made (a single husband carved it out of rock after his wife asked for a potato cellar).

Mount Aragats:

A dormant volcano.

A centre for climbing activities.

Byurakan:

An hour from Yerevan.

Byurakan Observatory.

Amberd Fortress is also very close by.

Mount Ararat:

The peak is now no longer within Armenian territory, but can be accessed and seen from here.

The Upper Azat Valley:

An hour's drive East from **Yerevan**.
One of **Armenia's World Heritage Sites** and the location of the incredible **Geghard Monastery.**

Dilijan National Park:
Possibly the best of four national parks. - lots of **Monasteries**.
But also amazing scenery and the rivers **Aghestev and Getik** both run through this fantastical area.

Sevan Lake:
The home of many monasteries but **Sevanavank Monastery** is one of the best to explore.
Sevan Bay is a good place for beaching activities.

Shikahogh State Reserve:
In the south of the country.
On the border with **Iran** so don't get lost!
Such a vast area much of it has never been explored!

Sisian:
Karahunj - Armenia's Stonehenge, with a vengeance!
200 Massive stone tombs with 40 stones standing in a circle.

Ani - Ani Ocakli:
Now within the neighbouring Turkish border.
A large area - abandoned **Armenian Village**.
There are **Caves** - a guide may be useful.

Steer clear of the troubled disputed area of **Nakhchivan** in the south west of the country.

The Republic of Azerbaijan:

Possibly better to enter from **Georgia** rather than **Armenia** due to current disputes.

Avoid Nagorno Karabakh.

Obtain a visa before entry - can be done easily when travelling, on line or from the U.K. can only stay easily for two weeks.

https://evisa.com.az/#

https://evisa.com.az/azerbaijan-transit-visa#:~:text=Trav elers%20are%20required%20to%20get,the%20best%2 0option%20for%20you.

Currency:

The **Manat** is the unit of currency here. It is divided into 100 **Gapiks**.
Currently 2 Manat are worth around £1.00.
Strangely, approximately 2 Manat are worth 1 U.S. Dollar.

Famous for Grand Prix car racing.

Places of interest:

Baku:
Capital City.

A good centre to tour from.

A typical modern and thriving town and **Harbou**r on the **Caspian Sea**.

There are some fantastic buildings to marvel at and all of the normal shopping and entertainment venues.

Yanar Dağ or **"Burning Mountain"**:

A natural glowing fire burning on a hillside along the **Caspian Sea**.

Sheki:

On the old **Silk Road**.

In the midst of the **Caucasus Mountains**.

A must not miss visit!!

In the town of **Sheki** you will find the most amazing, intact and still working **Caravanserai**.

Located inside the **Sheki Karvansaray Hotel**.

The doors are massively high to allow camels laden with goods from the east to enter.

Inside you will find comfort for the travellers.

An immense fire and seating.

There is wonderful architecture to be found here.

Visit the **Sheki Khans Palace**.

The town of **Sheki** is unlike anything you may have come across before which is why it is a **Unesco Heritage Site**.

Qobustan:

Mud volcano:

Prehistoric rock carvings and ancient graffiti.

Icheri Sheher:
Historic walled city
Shirvan National Park.

In order to travel further east, take the ferry over the **Caspian Sea** to **Aktau** in **Kazakhstan** - the departure ports are in **Baku** or **Alat**.

The buying of tickets is simple but there are no timetables.
The boat leaves when it is ready and there may be a three (or more) day wait.

https://www.madornomad.com/caspian-sea-ferry/#:~:text=Crossing%20the%20Caspian%20Sea%20by,to%20have%20a%20memorable%20experience.

https://en.wikivoyage.org/wiki/Ferries_in_the_Caspian_Sea

Alternatively take the coast road around the top of the **Caspian Sea** through **Georgia** and **Russia** which will take approximately 30 - 40 hours on a good week.
Bear in mind the close proximity of the current Ukraine/Russian conflict.

Best route to Tajikistan:

Baku or Alat - Azerbaijan
Ferry to:
Aktau - Kazakhstan
Tazhen/tajen border with Uzbekistan
Samarkand - Uzbekistan.
Dushanbe - Tajikistan.

Camping:

We are now entering the land of the **'Stans'**.
Kazakhstan, Kyrgyzstan, Uzbekistan, Turkmenistan, Tajikistan, Pakistan, Afghanistan and all of the minor **Stans**.

With regards to camping, whether it be campervan, motorhome, caravan, tent or just star watching, camp site facilities, where they can be found at all, will be very basic affairs, leaving you to care for yourselves.

You will probably need to dig your own latrines and provide your own food.
Bathing facilities are unheard of, leaving you to find a stream or use what water you may have brought with you.

Wild camping is much more to be expected and rewarded too.

There are many off the road areas that can be stopped in and just pitch up your tent or whatever.
Find a stream or lake for washing.

You may well be approached by locals wanting to get to know you.
Do not be concerned because these are friendly people and great friendships can be made by having an open house.

They may want to take you back home for a meal which is an excellent way to get to know a new culture.

As far as hotels or hostels go, these can only be found in the big cities which may be hundreds of miles away.

There is often a homestay available, with one or two makeshift bedrooms of sorts, which is the basic lodging house for a traveller.

These aren't always signposted but a villager will almost always be able to direct you to one locally.

Here you may or may not be offered a bed made with perhaps blankets or cushions and a meal, possibly breakfast too.

The Republic of Kazakhstan:

No visa required
30 day stay.
Proof of accommodation required.

The largest country in Central Asia.

The world's largest landlocked country, with Russia in the north, China in the east, Uzbekistan, Turkmenistan and Kyrgyzstan in the south and Georgia and the Caspian sea in the west.

Kazakhstan is greatly influenced by its Russian connections and historical ties.

Currency:

The **Tenge** is the unit of currency here. It is divided into 100 **tiyn**
Currently 1,000 Tenge are worth around £1.00.
Approximately 450 Tenge are worth 1 U.S. Dollar.

Places of interest:

Travelling from the west to the east.

Aktau:
A Port - A very pretty town.
Close to **Altyn-Emel National Park.**
Botanical Gardens.

Great place for walking on smart lawns, shopping, theatres, museums, there is even a puppet theatre and a skating rink.

Beyneu:
There's not much here but it's a convenient stopping place - 5 Hours from **Actau.**
Hotel Aknur is one of the better hotels with a 'vaguely' English speaking manager.
3 - 5000 tenge a night per room. (£3 - 5)

Aralsk:
A dried up **Aral sea.**
Some boats and other aquatic paraphernalia lay on a desert scene.
This was once a vast lake - A thriving fishing and canning industry.
The 4th largest lake in the world.
60 years of intensive agriculture and pollution by the Soviet authorities have left virtually nothing but a dried up desert.

Baikonur:
A centre for Russian space exploration.
Yuri Gagarin was sent into space from here.

Lake Balkhash:
Next to **The Ili River -** One of the largest lakes in Asia.
It is split into two halves.
Amazingly one half is fresh water and the other half is brackish.

The lake is very warm with little shade.
Swimming is possible.

Almaty:
Ile Alatau National Park.
Turgen Gorge.
Kayrak, Medvezhy and Skalisty Waterfalls.

Around 200,000 hectares in size - that's huge!

To give you some idea of its size - **Wales** in the U.K. is 2,000,000. Hectares.

There is an ancient road that runs along the spurs of the **Zailiysky Alatau.**
It was along this road that the silk road had its roots.
Turgen Gorge is in the east and The **Chemolgan River** is in the west.
The National Park borders **Almaty Nature Reserve.**
Bird watching is a must and there are over 30 species of wild animal to be found here including:
The Brown Tien Shan Bear, the Snow Leopard, Turkestan Lynx, stone marten and Indian Porcupine.

Lake Kaindy:
One of the best spots in **Kazakhstan** and must be on every travellers 'without fail' list.
It sits within **Kolsai Lakes National Park.**
Famous for the winter swims that are braved by hundreds each year.
Great for fishing too!

Rainbow trout and loach abound.
Watch out for the slim sunken lengths of the spruce trees rising up from the depths.

Tup - Karkara Valley:
Huge herds of wild horses, sheep and cows.
Be sure to sample local mare's milk called **Kumys**, which is a traditional drink in **Central Asia**.
It is known for its healing virtues and said to be an efficient remedy against tuberculosis, anaemia, gastro-intestinal diseases and much more.

Zharkent:
On the China International border.
Very much influenced by its Chinese neighbour.
If you want a taste of China this will be a good place to experience that.

When locals on either side of the border talk of **Khorgos**, they're most often referring to the **International Center for Border Cooperation (ICBC),** a special duty-free and visa-free shopping zone set up in the no-man's-land between the 2 countries.
Kazakhs call it by its Russian initials, MTSPS, pronounced as one word like **"EmTsePess"**.

This is as far east as we can go without a Chinese driving licence.
Travellers may enjoy travelling further east by other means.

Or explore the borders travelling south in **Kyrgyzstan** and **Tajikistan**.....

Our route will resume from **Beyneu** and the western border with **Uzbekistan**.

It is also possible at the moment to cross into **Uzbekistan** via the **Dostyk** border crossing.

The Republic of Uzbekistan:

No visa required for up to 30 days.

But can only transit for less than 3 days without registering.

See below:

Steer clear of **Termez** and the **Afghanistan** border.

Mediterranean climate.
Long hot summers.
Very hot in mid summer.

If you are a tourist transiting **Uzbekistan** in a recreational vehicle or staying in tents/camping, you are responsible for your own registration.

You should register online via the electronic registration system, *Emehmon, within* three days of arrival.

During the online registration process there will be a tourist tax charge for each day of your stay.

At the moment tourist tax can only be paid online by Uzbek debit card in local currency, therefore you should seek assistance from hotels or local tour operators.

Currency:

The **Som** is the unit of currency here.
This is divided into 100 Tiyin
Currently 1,500 Som are worth around £1.00.
11.5,000 soms are equivalent to one U.S. dollar

Accommodation:

Hotel - around £ 3 - 6.00. Per night.

Places of interest:

Muynak or Moynaq:
A dried up Aral sea.
Amu Darya River or **The Oxus** as it was known -
diverted and drying up.

Khiva:
Essentially an open-air museum.
There are over 50 historical sites in its tiny **Old Town.**
It is Central Asia's very first **UNESCO World Heritage City!**
Khiva resembles an ancient sandcastle town.
Do not miss **Tosh Hovli Palace**.
This is an exceptional place with no less than 150 rooms!!
Imagine what life was like during the times of the Khan's.

Bukhara - Ancient and modern religious culture.

Samarkand:
One of the oldest cities in the world.
Became very wealthy during the times of the old silk road.
Excellent for shopping, relaxing, walks and guided tours.
Souvenirs and museums.
A city once travelled to by droves during the Hippy culture of the 1960's.

Jizzakh:
Zaamin National Park:
Overwhelmingly beautiful scenery and wildlife.
Home to much wild life and many endangered species.
Apricot orchards, juniper forest and alpine meadow.
The Aldashmansoy, Baikungur, Guralsh and Kulsoy Rivers also flow through it.
Many spectacles await at the **Visitor Centre.**
Not to mention food of all descriptions.
Try the shish kebabs!
Then journey a little further over nearby **Suffa Pass,** where **Kyrgyz Nomads** camp.
Watch out for bearded vultures, Turkestan lynx and Asian black bears.
I hope you haven't forgotten your binoculars!
You will also find caves and gorges with footprints of dinosaurs.

Tashkent:
Uzbekistan's capital city.
One of the largest cities in central Asia.
Very hot in summer but mild during winter.

Lots of bazaars but don't miss **Chorsu Bazaar.**
Visit the **Drunken Duck** buffet restaurant. - All you can
eat and it is very welcoming.
Many Mosques and parks.
Shopping, theatres and galleries.
A three course meal in a good restaurant will set you
back around £15.00.

Kokand:
One of the most ancient cities.
Palace of Khudáyár Khán.

Ferghana Valley:
Home to **the Naryn** and the **Kara Daryan Rivers.**
Very fertile valley in the east.
On the route between **Kashgar in China** and
Samarkand - the old silk road.

Warning:
This is not an area much frequented by tourists and is a
mix of different, often warring nomads with differing
cultures and allegiances.

This is not a place of shopping arcades and guided
tours but a good place to make friends with the locals
and to 'muck in'.

There have been very recent vicious clashes in this area
between the locals and Kyrgyzstan and also with each
other so be aware of the potential for hostilities.

Margilan:
Yodgorlik Silk Factory:
This is a free tour. Excellent.

Fergana City:
A good base for travelling from to visit the local villages.
Taxis are virtually free or at least, extremely cheap.

Turkmenistan:

You will need a visa and a letter of invitation, possibly from a tour guide agency, to enter.

Currency:

The **New Manat** is the unit of currency here. It is divided into 100 **Tenge.**
Currently 500 New Manat are worth around £1.00.
Approximately 400 New Manat are worth 1 U.S. Dollar.
Watch out for the old Manat.
The currency was devalued in 1993 and new coinage was introduced.

From the coast of Turkmenistan to Merv (near Mary) on the silk road, are not restricted areas.

Places of interest:

Ashgabat:
The capital city of **Turkmenistan**.
Known for its **White Marble Buildings**.
There is a **Cable car** a short drive south (ask the taxi to wait).
This is an excellent way to see **Iran** without the fuss of getting a visa, as the top section, where there is a restaurant, is actually within the Iranian border.
National History Museum.
Interesting **Hippodrome**.
Watch the **Akhal-Teke** horses race**.**

Tolkuchka Bazaar - On the outskirts of **Ashgabat -** The biggest bazaar you have ever entered!
Anything can be bought here, from bananas to camels.
There is also a **Russian Bazaar** in the centre of town with the same name.
Do not confuse the two.

Bagyr:
Parthian Fortresses of Nisa - A UNESCO World Heritage Site.

Merv is an oasis city.
Here you will find an ancient fortress also dating from the Parthian era.

Darvaza:
In the **Karakum Desert** - A three hour drive from **Ashgabat**.
A Very Hot and burning gas crater, known as *'the gates of hell'*.
It is the only one in the world.

Gokdepe Museum:
Built to commemorate the first and second battle with Russia circa 1879 - 1880.
There is also a mosque inside the fortress.

Kow-ata:
Fantastic underground lake.
There is a distinct smell of sulphur here and they don't recommend that you swim for more than 20 minutes.

Yangykala:

Canyon - Approximately six hours drive west from **Ashgabat**.

Very difficult and arduous task to reach here.
Over sand dunes and extremely rough terrain.
Not for the fainthearted at all!

Kyrgyzstan:

No visa required
The people are very pleasant and friendly.
Some unsettled areas.
See the bazaars!!

Kyrgyzstan is at present at war with Tajikistan and so crossing borders between these two countries is 'interesting'.
But there are plenty of other access routes from neighbouring countries.

Currency:

The **Som** is the unit of currency here.
Currently 120 Som are worth around £1.00.
Approximately 90 Som are worth 1 U.S. Dollar.

Places of interest:

Bishkek, in the north, is the capital town.
In 1825 the **Khan** of **Kokand,** who's palace is now in **Uzbekistan,** established a clay fort here called **Pishpek**.
This is a great place to book tours from to see the rest of the country with a guide.
Come to **Osh Bazaar**! The largest in town.

If you are coming across from **Karkara** in **Kazakhstan** the first place of interest will be the immense lake - **Issyk Kul** - The name means **'Warm Lake'** and for good reason.

There are no less than 20 species of fish in the lake so a good day's fishing to be had.

The lake is surprisingly salty and one can actually float on it just like the **Dead Sea** in **Israel**.

It was from this area, In 1338, that the black death spread across the world.

Jety-Oguz Canyon:

Just a short drive west from **Karakol** *(not to be confused with Karakul in Tajikistan)*.

Famous for the huge red bulls that were bred here.

Issyk-Kul Spas - Below the cliffs is one remaining spa pool, there were several here.

Chunkurchak Gorge:

Far from the throng of tourists.

A gem of a place.

Beautiful colours and vivid scenery - Excellent!

Chon Kemin Valley:

Ancient burial mounds, horse riding, swimming, climbing, lakes, flora and fauna, mountain climbing, skiing, camping, yurting, hiking, rafting, pure beauty, you name it and here it will be found.

Travelling south from the capital for 45 minutes we come across **Ala Archa National Park** and **Gorge.**

I love these national parks, they are so vast!!
This one is filled with the most beautiful **Juniper Trees.**
As always, the wildlife is amazing too.
Here we can find Argali sheep, lynx, snow leopard, marten, Ibex and fox.
And for bird spotters there are golden eagle, bearded vulture, and Himalayan snowcock to name just a few.
As for mountains, you won't fail to miss the huge **Kyrgyz Alatau Range,** including **Korona Peak** (4,860 m) and **Semenov Tian Shansky** (4,895 m), both higher than anything found in Europe.

Tash Rabat:
A very beautiful valley.
The home of an ancient **Silk Road Caravanserai** - you can't fail to see it as you journey along the silk road.

In the south of the country is **Arslanbob.**
Beautiful mountains and famed for its walnuts - come walnut picking in the autumn!!

Osh is a little further south.
This is the second largest city.
Supposedly founded by all sorts of people from Alexander the Great to King Solomon.
Don't miss the very busy **Jayma Bazaar.**
It is spread out along the river banks.

Tajikistan:

Maximum stay - 60 days
An e visa is for 45 days.
An e visa cannot be extended.

Visa or e visa is required.
Visa fees for 3 months cost £ 115.00.

May be best to get one from a local Tajikistan embassy.

The Tajikistan embassy in:

Uzbekistan is in Tashkent
In Turkey is in Ankara
In Azerbaijan is in Baku
In Kazakhstan is in Astana

https://www.evisa.tj/index.evisa.html#/

Caravanistan.com can help with visas that are stuck or delayed.

For an e visa it's evisa.t and not visa.gov.t

A KBAO permit may also be required.
KBAO is an abbreviation for Kuhiston Badakhshan Autonomous Province of Tajikistan. (Around the Afghan border)
(Khorugh, Darvoz, Vanj, Rushon, Ishkoshim and Murghab. Additional fee is £ 15.00.

If you travel to Khatlon areas - Panj and Kamangir, you will need a permit from the Consular department of the Tajik Ministry of Affairs in Dushanbe.

You can also apply for a visa extension from here too.

Do not overstay the visa date.
But if you do, the friendly police will help you
through the court procedure.

It seems there is no limit to the amount of times you may leave and return on a new evisa.

It might also be possible to get a multiple entry visa.

See border info on caravanistan.com

Not friendly borders. - may be closed at short notice.

There is a useful Itinerary on againstthecompass.com

Useful sites: visagenie.co.uk

See entry requirements on
gov.uk/foreign-travel-advice/tajikistan

In **Tajikistan,** compared with neighbouring countries, the quality of diesel fuel is rumoured to be low, take an extra canister and refuel only at Gazprom stations

In the **Pamir** regions diesel can be blackmarket, diluted with paraffin and of a bad quality.
A filter may be useful.

Very hot summers so visits in August - to October are best.

Accommodation:

Wild camping is ok anywhere and campsites.
Hostels are available at around £7.00. Per night
Homestay is the equivalent of our bed and breakfast.
A hotel per night will cost around £ 10 to £ 30.00.

Currency:

The **Somoni** is the unit of currency here.
It is subdivided into 100 dirhams.
Currently 14 Somoni are worth around £1.00.
Approximately 11 Somoni are worth 1 U.S. Dollar.

Places of interest:

Konibodom:
A good border crossing junction to or from **Uzbekistan.**

Iskanderkul:
Iskander means Alexander and Kul means lake.
Close by - 43 metre waterfall **Fan Niagara**

Hilsor/Hisor/Hissar Fortress.

Dushanbe is a secure Town - Afghan border area.

Garam Chashma - Khorog - Hot springs. 42 km south of **Khorog**

Jelondy - Spa and hot springs.

Khargush:
Some 30 Kms before the military checkpoint at **Khargush** (border with Afghanistan).
Riverside, yaks, camels, colourful ladies.

Wakhan Corridor Nature Reserve:
is on the border with **Afghanistan**.

Murghab and **Khorugh - Tajik National Park:**
There are brown bear, snow leopards, Marco Polo sheep, Indian geese, various local fish and Siberian ibex
Karakul Lake:
Here you can fish, climb, trek, horse ride and even camel ride if you prefer.

To travel further eastwards one must enter either China, Russia or Afghanistan.

It may be possible to employ a driver to transport a vehicle through China.
Owning a Chinese driving licence is compulsory.

To reach Pakistan and India you must travel through north Afghanistan.

Possibly at **Shir Khan Bandar** or **Gulbahor** in the north through **Kabul** to **Torkham (Khybar pass)** near **Peshawar** in the south. (14 hours).

Although some tour operators travel these routes it is not advised in the present climate.

For tours and advice on visiting Afghanistan, Pakistan, Iran, Iraq and Syria please go to: againstthecompass.com

Northern Europe:

Too cold - don't go there.

Middle Europe:

Holland: - The Netherlands.

Schengen rules apply.
90 day maximum stay in E.U. applies.

A country of daffodils and canals, cheeses, clogs and windmills.

The Netherlands rebranded their country as recently as 2020.
Formerly it was known as Holland.
However, Holland was a description of a large area known since the days of **Napoleon** for its contribution to the war at that time.
Holland was principally the area covered by the northern towns.
The Netherlands is now hoping to increase the popularity of other areas by changing its name.

Apparently, it is still o.k. to refer to the country as Holland.

Holland is known for being a very flat, low country, hence the reason for bicycles being extremely popular.

Much of its coastline has been reclaimed from the **Zuiderzee** by the very clever use of **Dykes** and **Polders**.

Famed for the boy, known as **Hans Brinker,** the author of the story, who once stuck his finger in a leaking dyke and so saved all of **Holland** from drowning.

Also for **Van Gogh, Rembrandt** and **Vermeer** amongst many others.

Curiously, **Anthony Van Dyke**, who many assume to be Dutch, was Flemish, born in **Antwerp**, which was then a part of the Spanish Netherlands and is now in Belgium.

Most people speak English in **Amsterdam.**

An interesting fact is that, on average, the Dutch are the tallest people in the world.

It is sometimes worth remembering that at one time most of Holland was under water.

Holland is famous for its cheeses:
Gouda cheese is the most famous, and most produced. There is also Dutch Cheese, followed by Edam, Maasdam, Boerenkaas, Leyden and many lesser known cheeses.

You may come across a very Dutch drink called **Jenever** - do not enter into a debate as to its similarity to Gin.

The colour orange is favoured here, being the colour adopted by the royal family.

William of Orange, or William the Silent, the first William is to be thanked for this.

It was William the third, his grandson, who eventually became king of England and overthrew the Catholic King James second, much to the relief of many protestants in Northern Ireland and is celebrated to this day by the marching bands of the 'Orangemen'.

Places of interest:

We must begin with **Amsterdam:**

Amsterdam:
Famed worldwide for its flowers and cheese markets.
Visit **Anne Frank's House** and the **Van Gogh Museum**.
One of the best cities to experience **Canal Cruises.**

Zaanse Schans:
An area with an awful lot of very famous windmills.
Very typical of Holland's landscape.
Very photogenic.

The Hague:
This is the seat of the Dutch government and home to the Royal Family.
One of the world's most expensive cities.

Zoeterwoude:
Heineken Beer.
Come for a tour of the factory.

Delft:
Famed for its **Pottery** and **Vermeer artwork.**

Rotterdam:
'The Dam of the River Rotte'.
A very modern city with very tall buildings.

Gouda:
This is the place to experience **'Cheese'.**
There is a very interesting **Historic Town Hall** building too.
Good for a day trip.

De Haar:
The largest castle in Holland.
This is the sometime residence of the **Van Zuylen** family who are renowned for inviting very famous, and infamous, guests for wild parties and revelries.

Luxembourg:

Schengen rules apply.
90 day maximum stay in E.U. applies.

A landlocked country.

Languages are Luxembourgish, French and German.
English is also widely spoken as is Portuguese.

Its capital city is called Luxembourg.

Places of interest:

Luxembourg:
The capital.
See the **Grand Dukes Palace.**

Vianden - Victor Hugo's Museum and **Vianden Castle.**

Meer van Echternach:
Extremely beautiful lake with park land.
There is also a **Roman Villa.**
The **Abbey of Echternach** and close by the **Gorges du loup -** possibly one of Luxembourg's best bits!

Belgium:

Schengen rules apply.
90 day maximum stay in E.U. applies.

Belgium has three official languages.
French, Dutch and German.
Wallon, which is also widely spoken, is a variant of the
French language.

Famous for beers, chocolates and waffles.
Oh, and of course, Poirot, the famous detective.

Did you know that French fries actually come from
Belgium??

Places of interest:

We will begin with the most well known spots.

Bruges:
A mediaeval city, visit the **13th Century Belfry.**
Canals and cobbled streets. Very picturesque.

Antwerp:
The place to visit for **Jewellery -** known as the diamond
capital of the world.
It is also one of the major sea ports.
Anthony Van Dyke the very famous *Dutch* artist was
born here.

Brussels:
The capital of Belgium and the seat of the European Union parliament.

The Sonian Forest - 4,000 acres of woodlands.

Durbuy:
The smallest town on earth.
Cobbled streets and stone houses.

Dinant:
Away from the busy towns this is a picture of a place.
On the **River Meuse**.
Backed by sheer cliffs.
Great for wandering the streets and dining.

Vallee du Ninglinspo:
A river valley, great for long walks.

Eifel Nature Park:
Incredible wildlife – wild cats, wild boars, red deer, eagle owls, wildcats, black grouse and lynx have also been recently spotted here.

Spa:
Famous for being one of the original Spas thermal waters and hot springs.

The Federal Republic of Germany:

Schengen rules apply.
90 day maximum stay in E.U. applies.

Our route through Germany rather cleverly marks out the figure two on the map and ends on the Swiss border.

Places of interest:

Dresden:
If you enjoy ballroom dancing with all the glitz and glamour, you won't want to miss **Zwinger** in **Dresden.**

Berlin:
The capital city of Germany.
There is a somewhat eager desire to churn over the effects of the cold war here as the multitude of museums focussed on the subject will confirm.
History buffs will love it.
Take a quick look at **Checkpoint Charlie** whilst you're here.
There is an abundance of museums here and some are possibly the best in the world, but there are so many to choose from.
The Holocaust Memorial is a place to wonder and reflect, as is the **Berlin Wall.**
The **Brandenburg Gate** and also the **Cathedral** are worth seeing in order to tick them off the list.
The Tiergarten has 500 acres, yes, 500 acres, of parkland to relax in.

There is also a **Zoo** in **Berlin** with an impressive reintroduction program but that is not in the **Tiergarten**, despite its name.

The Glass Dome of The Reichstag is pretty impressive.

The KonzertHaus - Is where to go for ballet, opera, theatre and music.

Not forgetting, of course, the food and also the night life. **Berlin** never sleeps. - Anything is possible - Take a ride in a **Trabbie car.**

Hamburg:

Not to be missed!

Miniatur Wunderland - The world's largest miniature railway.

The Port is a great place to begin to discover this great town.

Find a guide and take a walking tour of the city to get your bearings and discover something of its history and present wonders.

The Elbtunnel is a great way to cross under the river. The tunnel closes at 7 p.m. entry is by **Bridge 6** in **Landungsbrücken**

Hanover:

Interestingly, **Hanover** was once a part of the **U.K.** The present royal family are descended from Hanovarian stock.

Much of **Hanover** was demolished during the second world war.

This is a very green city with a lot of parks.

Be sure not to miss **The Maschsee -** an artificial lake.
The Stadtpark.
The Great Garden.
Eilenriede the Great Hannover Woods.
The Hermann-Löns Park and the **Zoo.**

Bremen:
Sits on the **Weser River.**
Visit the old town for local goodies.
The Town Hall is well worth visiting.
Take a look at the **Roland Statue**, symbolic of the city's freedom.

Cologne:
On the **Rhine** - so beautiful.
Twin towered **Cathedral** and Gothic architecture.
Lindt Schokoladen Museum - Chocolate Museum.
Yummy.

Bonn:
The Rhine - Take a cruise down the **Rhine.**
Here at **Bonn** is the most glamorous stretch of water.
Bundeskunsthalle - Art gallery

Frankfurt:
A key stopping place when travelling along the **Rhine**
from **Switzerland**, travelling north and vice versa.
Famous for?? You got it - **Frankfurter Sausages.**
The Stadel Museum is filled to the brim with very famous art works. - well worth visiting.

Karlsruhe:
This is where the **Black Forest** proper begins and journeys all the way south to **Switzerland**.
There are some great hikes and trekking to be done.

Baden Baden:
The place to go for a spa.
The Romans discovered spas in this area some two thousand years ago,

Stuttgart:
A good place for wine tasting.
There is also a **Chocolate Exhibition,** a **Dinosaur museum, Wilhelma Zoological and Botanical Gardens,** with some 8000 animals and over 6000 different species of plants and do not miss the **Mineral Springs.**

Munich:
Pinakothek der Moderne - A very modern art gallery.
The Octoberfest - as its name might suggest, is a beer festival held in October.
Don't forget your 'lederhosen'!

Berchtesgaden National Park:
On the Austrian border.
While you are here, visit the **Salt Mines**.

Neuschwanstein - Fairytale Castle - Children and adults will love it.

Lake Constance:
Shared with both **Switzerland** and **Austria**.
A panoramic vision of grace and beauty.
Superb place to just relax and rest after all of that sightseeing.

The Principality of Liechtenstein:

Participates in the Schengen area.
Not in the E.U.

Due to its geographical location the 90 day maximum stay in E.U. applies.

The language here is mostly German.

One of the world's smallest countries but also the world's richest due to its attractive corporation and other tax laws.

Places of interest:

Vaduz is the capital city.
Vaduz Castle - The palace and official residence of the Prince of Liechtenstein.

Balzers - Gutenberg Castle. - Guided tours are available.

The Federal Parliamentary Republic of Austria:

Schengen rules apply.
90 day maximum stay in E.U. applies.

If you use Austrian motorways 'Autobahn' and 'S' roads you must display a motorway vignette sticker on the inside of the windscreen of your vehicle as you enter Austria.

Failure to have one will mean a heavy, on-the-spot fine.

You can get a motorway vignette at all major border crossings into Austria and at larger petrol stations.

All vehicles above 3.5 tonnes maximum permitted laden weight using motorways and expressways must have a small device - called the **'GO-BOX '** - attached to the windscreen.

Food:

Sarma - Can also be eaten in Turkey, Armenia, Azerbaijan, Iran, Greece, Bulgaria, Romania, Moldova, and Serbia.
But it is said that Austrian Sarma is the best.

From Vienna to Innsbruck, Austria is full of history, culture and beauty.

Places of interest:

Our route travels west from Vienna towards Lake Constance.

Vienna:

The capital city, in the east of the country, is where we will begin our journey.

Ride the **Danube.**

There are copious opportunities to listen to **Mozart, Lintz, Beethoven, Strauss** and others here.

Find out all there is to know about **Charlemagne** - The first *'Holy'* Roman Emperor.

Visit and tour **St Stephen's Cathedral.**

Come to **The Opera House.**

Schonbrunn & Belvedere Palaces

Take a tour of **The Hofburg Palace,** the home of the **Habsburgs.**

Vienna Woods:

South west from **Vienna.**

Here there be wild boar and badgers, as well as roe deer and many other creatures and birds.

Krems:

A beautiful mediaeval city set in the wonderful fertile valley of **Wachau.**

A good opportunity for that ride on the **Danube** and some more shopping.

Wachau:

On the banks of the **River Danube.**

Great for wine lovers and diners.

A cultural hub and exciting city.
Also visit - **Jauerling Wachau Nature Park.**
Within an hour from **Vienna.**
Absolutely stunning!
A must not miss excursion.

Linz:

On the **Danube** with excellent architecture to marvel at.
Cobbled streets and chilling over coffee.
Lots of very famous colleges and art museums. - Very cultural.

Salzburg:

The shooting location for **The Sound of Music** - *you might remember that one?* And the birthplace of **Mozart** (the musician).
What more could you want from a town?
Well, there is more **- The Fortress Hohensalzburg.**
One of the largest mediaeval fortresses in Europe.
Mirabell Palace - take the tour and see the gardens.
fantastic!
Salzburg is filled with beautiful gardens.
The best time to go is after the crowds have left during Autumn.

Hallstatt:

A village on **Lake Hallstatt's** western shore in **Austria's** mountainous **Salzkammergut** region.
There are 16th-century **Alpine Houses** and alleyways, cafes and shops.

A **Funicular Railway** connects to **Salzwelten**, an ancient salt mine with a subterranean salt lake, and to **Skywalk Hallstatt** viewing platform.
A trail leads to the **Echern Valley Glacier Garden** with glacial potholes and **Waldbachstrub Waterfall**.

Eisriesenwelt Cave:
Wow! Just Wow!
The largest **Ice Cave** in the world - imagine.
Take the cable car ride for a must see visit but if you are not in a hurry, do the trek.
Well worth the effort.

Bad Gastein:
Mountains and snow.
In truth, **Bad Gastein** isn't so bad at all.
Excellent for skiing and climbing.
You won't want to miss the **Gasteiner Waterfall**.
Famed for its hot thermal springs.
Take a dip.

Zell Am See:
Meaning Zell by the lake.
A beautiful, picturesque little town by the lake **Zell**.
Mountainous area.
Don't forget to travel the **Cable Car** to the top for a fine view.

Grossglockner High Alpine Road:
A 'Hold on to your Knickers' drive!
Between **Zell Am See** and **Dölsach**.

The whole ride is both terrifying and beautiful.

Krimml Waterfalls:
So much water!!
Such a paradise of scenery.
Great for trekking and just relaxing too.

Swarovski Kristallwelten:
A **Park** and an **Art Museum**.
Quite artistic and beautiful.

Innsbruck:
Famed for winter skiing and summer hiking.
Schloss Ambras Castle was, and is, the first museum
in the world.
Well worth a wander round, quite fascinating.

Vorarlberg:
More Wonderful Mountains!
Great skiing spot.

Bregenz – Lake Constance.

*We will now return to **Vienna** and travel south towards
Carinthia.*

*You may prefer to backtrack from **Bregenz**, pick up
Carinthia on the way, to finish your journey back in
Vienna.*

Neusiedler See-Seewinkel National Park:
Great wildlife spot.
Here you might see the **Russian Tarantula!** Toads,
horses, donkeys, Hungarian longhorns, and water
buffalos all grazing wild.
And for us tweeters there are sea eagles, great
bustards, various herons, various bee-eaters, and
spoonbills.
Lake Neusiedl is the largest endorheic lake in Central
Europe.

Eisenstadt:
Visit the **Esterházy Palace.**
The gardens alone are worthy of the visit but the palace
is marvellous.
Also in the palace is an interactive **Hyden Exhibition**
which is really one of a kind and brings the musician into
reality.
One can also visit **Haydns House** and the
Österreichisches Jüdisches Museum.
There is also a must see **Austrian Jewish Museum,**
which can be quite an emotional event.

Graz:
The centre of **Styria,** the 'green heart' of Austria. -
Immerse yourselves In history, culture, and food

Worthersee:
If you enjoy swimming, this lake is for you.
There is also canoeing and windsurfing, water skiing, in
fact just about any water sport you might think of is here.

This is one of Austria's top summer destinations and when you've dried out visit the cool **Griffen Stalactite Cave.**

There are also cathedrals to inspire and museums to pass the time in.

Plus loads and loads of restaurants, coffee houses, and shops.

And now we have arrived at the wonderful region of **Carinthia.**

On the **Slovenian** border - Lakes, mountains, hiking, skiing and chilling.

Austria is filled with so much natural beauty, there are surprises around each and every corner.

There are **Three National Parks** that you must not miss:

National Park Donau Auen.
National Park Gesause.
Nationalpark Hohe Tauern.

Styria - Southern province of Austria - filled with natural forest and wildlife.

Burgenland – A western province within Austria - snow and mountains.

Mostviertel - The southwestern quarter of the four quarters of **Lower Austria.**

It is bordered on the north by the **Danube** and to the south and west by the state borders of **Styria** and **Upper Austria** respectively.

Here you can find wonders such as **Melk Abbey** and **Aggstein Castle** amongst the many others we have already mentioned.

Tyrol - Austria western state, in the heart of the **Alps** which also overlaps into **Italy.**

Switzerland:

Switzerland is not a member of the E.U. or the E.E.A. but is part of the single market.

Schengen rules apply.

90 day maximum stay in E.U. applies.

Ok for driving - do not need a permit if you have a U. K. driving licence and live in the U.K.

You will need snow chains.
The standard yellow triangle.
A motorway sticker if you intend to travel on motorways.
A U.K. sticker on the rear of your vehicle or incorporated within your number plate (Not a G.B. sticker).

It is probably worth buying a **Swiss travel pass** here to give free admittance to many places and free rides or discounts on transport.

Places of interest:

Bern:
Has a mediaeval town centre.
Very quaint.
It is famed for the **Lindt Chocolate Factory.**
At the age of 23 **Albert Einstein** decided to take up residency here.

His most famous work - **The Special Theory of Relativity** was published at **Bern.**

There are many **Free Outdoor Pools** which is something of a bonus during the warm summer days.

The **Gantrisch Nature Park** will keep you busy for hour upon hour.

Bears are the animal of favour in **Bern** - hence its name.

You will see them everywhere.

It is said that the city was founded by one of these animals.

But the truth is a little more grizzly.

Taste **Emmental Cheese**, hike, enjoy the outdoors, eat and visit the town's many museums.

Lausanne:

On the beautiful **Lake Geneva.**

French is the most widely spoken language here.

On the lake shore there is **the International Olympic Committee Headquarters,** as well as the **Olympic Museum** and **Lakeshore Olympic Park.**

The city itself, like much of **Switzerland**, has mediaeval streets with a **12th-century Gothic Cathedral**.

19th-century Palais de Rumine.

Cantonal Fine Art and **Science Museums.**

Geneva:

Home of the **Geneva Convention** - A well laid out and documented agreement that altered nothing.

The headquarters for very many international organisations.

Geneva is a bit of an international financial centre.
A very scenic town with the **Swiss Alps** overlooking.
Plenty of fine museums.
Don't miss the **Geneva Water Fountain.**
St. Pierre Cathedral.
Palais de nations.

Chillon Castle:
Home to the **Counts of Savoy** during the 16th century.
Built in the 1300's one of the best preserved mediaeval castles anywhere.

Gruyere - Gruyere Castle and **Cheese.**
Very picturesque landscape.
Rolling hills and green grass.
Gruyere Castle is well worth a visit.
Romance and chivalry seep from its walls.
There are some great views from the battlements too!
Taking a tour of the **Cheese Factory** is a must of course.
Maison Cailler is the **Chocolate Factory** where you can participate in a workshop. - so much fun!
Plus, A tour of **The Gruyere Lake** is something you might not expect.
Full of surprises. - A bit unusual.
Rock tunnels, waterfalls and woods.

Lake Thun:
Take a boat out on the lake for a day - Excellent choice.
Walk over **The Covered Bridge** and enjoy the very weird two tiered streets.

Thun Castle will keep you busy for two or three hours, Fascinating history of the town.

Don't miss viewing **The Panorama,** known as a **Cyclorama,** the world's oldest circular painting - it is massive!

It's housed in a specially-built round building at the **Thun Art Museum** in **Schadau Park.**

It gives an intimate look at life in **Thun** in the early 19th century.

Oberhofen Castle - built around 1200.

A tour of the lake has a stop off here so it's worth the ride.

Spiez:

Also on the lake and by boat is a good way to arrive.

Visit the **Castle** - there are so many in this area.

Lots of watersports to enjoy here as well.

If you take a hike into the mountains watch out for ibex, beavers, chamois, marmots and golden eagles.

St Beatus Caves - These caves have got to be on the 'not to miss' list.

There are rock formations created over millions of years deep under the ground.

A **Cave Museum** here too.

Interlaken:

Stunning **Alpine Peaks** just for a start off.

Very busy in summer but a completely different scene in winter.

The Bernese Alps:
The rooftop of Europe.
This trip is best travelled by railway.
The **Bernese Railway** is an ideal way to view the delicious passes, lakes and mountains.
These blue and yellow trains join **Interlaken Ost** with **Grindelwald** and **Lauterbrunnen.**
From the comfort of your railway carriage tour the peaks of the **Eiger, Jungfraujoch, Monch** and **Finsteraarhorn.**

The Lauterbrunnen Valley:
Known for its many waterfalls,
If you spend any time here at all you simply cannot miss **The Staubbach Waterfall.**
Particularly if you are strolling along the promenade in **Lauterbrunnen.**

Lake Lugano:
Very picturesque and great for easy hiking.
Lots of places to just sit and enjoy the scenery.
Parking isn't easy so here again, the boat is the way to go.

Ticino:
No less than two amazing lakes here, the **River Ticino** and at least **Two Castles!**
What more could a person need?
There is also an **Amusement Park** called **The Swissminiatur.**

A good way of getting about here is to take a ride on the **Lake Maggiore Express Train.**
Take your heart in your hands as you walk the **Tibetan Bridge Of Curzutt.**
This is a bridge walk you will not ever stop talking about.

The Castles of Bellinzona, the capital city of **Ticino** are a day trip to remember - A group of very well preserved fortifications.
Castello San Giorgio - 14th century castle owned by the very powerful **Gonzaga Family.**

Lucerne:
The covered **Chapel Bridge** is the one to aim for here.
Then sit back and enjoy the views.
Climb **Mt Pilatus** and **Mt. Rigi** and also enjoy a long leisurely boat ride around the lake.
But not all on the same day.
Altstadt - The old town is a great area to stroll around.
Allow a couple of hours if you're in a hurry.

Zurich:
The largest city in **Switzerland** and filled with city type activities.
A commercial centre.
Art works, drinking coffee, visiting museums and shopping.
Zurich has a **Zoo** for when you fancy a change of scenery.

There are over 500 clubs and bars here and a vibrant nightlife, but on the bright side, there is a free bike rental system and amazing public transport.

The watersports on the lake abound of course.

Take your pick as long as you don't mind becoming wet.

Schaffhausen:
Rhine Falls.
The most powerful waterfall in Europe no less.
Breathtaking and stupendous, are just a couple of adjectives that can describe it but, honestly, you have to experience this one!
This waterfall is immense!
It can be viewed from both sides, the north and the south.
We recommend that you visit from the south side, it is possible to get right up close, where there is a castle, **Schloss Laufen,** and a **Museum.**
The only downside to this is that there is a small fee, *CHF5* per person.

Beverin Nature Park:
An immense area including different cultures, languages and communities.
The home of the Ibex, amongst many other animals and birds.
For hiking you couldn't want better than the **Rofla Gorge** and the **Forest of Sounds.**

Whilst in the area, travel along the **San Bernardino Pass -** Not to be missed.

There are so many treks and rides, views and climbs.

Near **Flims:**
The Ruinaulta or **Rheinschlucht - Switzerland's Grand Canyon.**
On the edge of the park - A huge, massive, immense canyon on the **Rhine.**
It can be accessed on foot, over water, by train or by bike.
The Swiss are, quite rightly, not keen on motorised traffic spoiling their beautiful scenery.
You will need at least a full day's excursion here.
Or stop overnight in one of the fine hostelries close by.
It is possible to take a vehicle on the rough singletrack road along the edge of the gorge, but not recommended.

St. Moritz:
The resort of the rich and famous during the nineteen sixties.
Here there be **Mineral Springs.**
The, 'must go to' destination for skiers and followers of mountain sports.
Whether it is climbing, hiking, trekking, kayaking, canoeing, skiing, windsurfing, boating, fishing or scuba diving, this is the centre for all mountain and water sports.

Swiss National Park:
There is no fee to enter here and no fee for the information centre either.
There are no vehicles allowed in the park.
One of the first conservation centres in Europe.
The park is 66.5 square miles in size.
Romansh is widely spoken.

The Brusio Spiral Viaduct was built in 1908 near **Brusio** to solve the problem of getting trains up the hill in a limited amount of space, and without using tunnels that would block the views for tourists travelling on the **Bernina Railway.**
The track layout is hilarious!

You can still ride this route on the **"Bernina Express"** sightseeing train, it's got to be among the most scenic in the world.
It runs from **Chur (or Davos)** in Switzerland to **Poschiavo** in Switzerland and **Tirano** in Italy by crossing the **Swiss Engadin Alps.**

The Matterhorn:
Arguably the most famous of all the peaks, lies in both **Italy** and **Switzerland**.
Gornergrat is one of the highest viewpoints in the area to see the **Matterhorn.**
It is possible to take the train up from **Zermatt, Zermatt** is a car free town and so it will be necessary to get there by train from **Interlaken,** changing at **Visp** or **Spiez.**

It is also possible to take a train from **London England** at a cost of just over **£137.00.**

Hungary:

Is in the E.U.
Is in Schengen
There is a 90 day maximum stay.

On a direct route line from **Calais** to **Istanbul.**
Unless following the scenic route.

There are multiple troop movements within Hungary at the time of going to print.

Do not attempt to cross into Ukraine from Hungary.

One of the cheapest countries within Europe to buy fuel.

There is a **Budapest Card** available for discounted and free entry to various sites and transport.

Currency:

The Forint is the unit of currency here.
Currently 440 Forints are worth around £ 1.00.
Approximately 340 Forints are worth 1 U.S. Dollar.

Do not exchange money in airports - the rates are horrendous.
Cities tend to give the best rates or just bring your nil commission cash/credit card to use in the atm's.

Places of interest:

Budapest:

The capital city of Hungary.

Comprising two cities - **Buda** and **Pest.**

Budapest is bisected, (not dissected), by the **River Danube**.

Its 19th-century **Chain Bridge** connects **Buda,** which is hilly, with **Pest,** which is flat.

There is a **Funicular** that travels up **Castle Hill** to **Buda's Old Town**.

Budapest History Museum is a mine of information from Roman times onward.

Trinity Square is where a 13th-century **Matthias Church** sits.

Also **Fisherman's Bastion,** from where you will see some amazing views.

Don't miss the **Great Market Hall**.

Memento Park too is a must visit during the summer period.

In all, **Budapest** is one of the cheaper visits but also one of the best, so good value all round.

Particularly wonderful are the amazing **Baths** to soak in.

Whilst you are here please visit the enormous **Buda Castle - The Palace of the Kings**!

It was pillaged and bombed during ww2 sadly.

There are now no less than **Two Museums** housed within its walls.

A walking tour is advisable costing around £10.00.

Free admission is available with the **Budapest Card.**

From **Budapest** we shall begin our tour travelling northward along the **Danube River** and then turn west, touring **Hungary** in an anticlockwise direction.

Ending our tour on the far north eastern border with **Hungary's** neighbour, **Slovakia.**

Szentendre:
The perfect day trip, just 30 minutes from the capital.
An absolutely stunningly scenic village.
Winding and cobbled alleyways and tree lined streets.
Not much has changed here since its mediaeval heyday.
There are a couple of museums - **Margit Kovacs Ceramics Museum** and the **Ferenczy Museum.**
And art galleries to browse in - **The Art Mill, The Amos** and **Anna Museum.**
We are in a very artistic environment today.
During the afternoon, take a walk up the hill and admire the views of the superb **Danube River** swirling below.

Esztergom:
On the **Slovakian** border - Once the capital city of **Hungary.**
The Basilica:
Whilst this is but a church, it is worth mentioning for being the largest in **Hungary.**
It really is quite big.
I'm not sure who they were trying to impress but they certainly made their mark.
As for bigness - The altarpiece is a massive 13.5 X 6.6 metres in size, depicting the **Assumption of the**

Blessed Virgin Mary, by Girolamo Michelangelo Grigoletti and is the largest painting in the world, on a single canvass.

Visegrád Castle or **Citadel**:
Not to be confused with a castle of the same name in **Prague.**
This is quite a sight to see alongside the mighty **Danube River.**
Built in the 900's as a fortress, it was destroyed by the Mongol invasion of the 1240's but remains rebuilt and as bold as brass for all to see.
Parking is 500 HUF/h and there is a fee to enter the castle and museum, which I would imagine is fairly interesting for local history buffs.
After 6. p.m. parking is free and so is the view, which is what most people go for.

Győr - Still following the **Danube**:
There is a Zoo - **Xantus János.**
Very friendly locals and great food!
Baroque Architecture.
The town is definitely worth walking around for its quirky statues and ceramics museum.
Take a stroll around the old town which has some unique architecture and amazing alleys and shops.

Fertő-Hanság National Park:
Take a boat tour, either by canoe or solar powered boat
- fishing, bird watching - heron, marsh harriers,

white-tailed eagles and fauna and flora spotting too - many rare and endangered species.
This is a protected wetlands area.

Sopron:
Just one hour from **Vienna** here.
We have entered a great wine producing region, both red and white wines hail from this area.
The old town has cobbled streets and friendly shopkeepers.

Hévíz:
South of **Lake Balaton.**
A spa town with very warm natural spa waters.
Also home of the theme park **- Bobo.**

Tapolcai-tavasbarlang Látogatóközpont:
A vast **Lake Cave.**
A complex and enormous cave system running underneath the town of **Tapolcai.**
The adult fee is 3500 HUF with discounts and reductions but worth every single penny (or forint).

Lake Balaton:
If you go nowhere else in Hungary visit here!
Lake Balaton is a very special place.
The largest lake in central Europe.
Getting around the lake is easy either by boat, train or bus.
Lots of great beaches, towns and villages.

Uplands National Park:
If you're looking for lush green forests, sailing, swimming, biking, beaches, culture, food, hiking and more, this is the place for you.
Here you can eat *Lángos* to your heart's content.
With the warm shallow water lapping at your feet you will never want to leave.

Tihany:
Benedictine Tihany Abbey.
Dating back to the mid-11th century.
If you arrive at the right time of year, late June - early July, you will be overwhelmed by the smell of **Lavender** growing in the local fields.
While you are here, stop for a coffee and cake in the nearby **Rege Cukrászda.**
Do not park anywhere in **Tihany,** it's very expensive.
There are plenty of road stops along the circular route around the lake, or use public transport.

Siofok:
The Journey takes one hour on a ferry from **Tihany** or one hour to drive around the shoreline.
Siofok is the main town on the **Balaton Lakeside.**
Visit the watchtowers, chill out and do some fishing.

We are continuing south now to the town of:

Pécs:
On the sides of the **Mecsek Mountains.**

From **Széchenyi Square,** which was once the market square, walk around the city centre, to admire its architecture and people and to get a hang on the layout of this beautiful city.

You will find the **Mosque of Pasha Gazi Kasim** that is now a church and a **Cathedral** named after **Peter** and **Paul** and also a mosque that is still a mosque.

Even the synagogue here is immense.

If you are looking for art, here you will find many museums and art galleries to browse through.

Lake Tisza:
Water Chestnut Fields and **Lily Pads.**
A great wetland site.

Here you can find very inexpensive accommodation and shopping sites, restaurants etc.

Actually there are several lakes here and each one is another wonder.

Take a **Wild Water Tour** to discover some of the amazing wild bird colonies that exist in this place.

Grey Heron, Purple Heron, Little Egret, Great Egret, Squacco Heron and Little Bittern. Spoonbill, Great Cormorant and Common Tern, Black Stork. Black Kite, Saker Falcon and Eurasian Hobby.

Visit the aquarium at **Poroszlo.**

Eat enormous pancakes at **Abádszalók**

There are spas at **Berekfürdő, Tiszafüred** and **Tiszakécske.**

Hortobágy National Park - The Puszta:
A part of the **Great Plain** in **Eastern Hungary.**

This is the area that birthed **Attila the Hun!**
Now grazed by ducks, wild fowl, cows, sheep and horses for over two thousand years.
The Nine-Arch Bridge was created as a result of the annual flooding problem.
The Vernacular Barna-type Windmill was built in 1858.
The four-storey brick structure was built with a turning roof structure and four blades.
Visit the **Körszín Museum** to find out more about this wonderful area.

Debrecen:
A great centre for travelling from.
Visit the **Agora Science Centre, Kerekerdo Adventure Park.**
Don't miss a wander around the **Debrecen Zoo** and **Botanical Garden.**

Eger:
On the **Eger River**:
In the centre of town - **Eger Castle.**
An amazing history here where women fought alongside their menfolk against 60,0000 invading Ottomans and won (temporarily).
The **Istvan Dobó Castle Museum** is worth visiting whilst in the castle grounds - filled with interesting art and historical information on the castle.
A 30 minute walk southwest and you will find **The Valley of the Beautiful Women -** an excellent wine making

district, from where the red wine, **Bulls Blood,** comes from - a particular favourite of mine. Whilst it may take 30 minutes to walk to the wine vaults/caves, beware how much sampling is done as the way back may be tricky.
Város a Város Alatt -Take a tour underneath the city. Don't forget to swim in the open air, soothing and healing **Public Mineral Spa.**

Bükk National Park - In the **Bükk Mountain Range.** O.k. Before we begin, to be clear, the Hungarian spelling is **Bükki National Park** but as we are writing in English the translation here is correctly spelt **Bükk.**
I really don't wish to argue the case.
Just enjoy the park.
Here, there are **Hanging Gardens and Szalajka Valley** including, but not limited to, **The Veil Waterfall.** You can view the 20 metres high waterfall on **Szinva Stream.**
You will discover enormous and fantastic caves and lakes, forests and wildlife like never before.
Great for hikes, treks and more serious explorations.

Miskolc-tapolca - Cave Bath - Technically a theme park now, which includes a boating lake and subterranean swimming in **Miskolctapolca Cave Bath,** an aquatic centre with naturally heated pools.
Miskolctapolca Adventure Park has treetop rope trails, and the raised, year-round **Miskolc Bobsled Toboggan Track.**

Lillafüred:

We mentioned hanging gardens and caves earlier?

Well here they are:

The **Hotel Palota** on the top of a steep hill is our starting point.

P.s. Don't miss the flora and fauna in your rush to visit the caves, take time to walk around these amazing gardens.

From here, you can walk to the **Anna Cave** and the statue of one of Hungary's best known poets, **Attila József.**

The 20-metre Waterfall, which is created by the **Szinva Stream** coursing into **Miskolc** from **Felső-Hámor.**

Lake Hámor is fed by the **Garadna** stream.

The Anna Cave is next, which is a limestone cave created not by water erosion but by limestone building up on the walls.

St. Stevens Cave is caused by **Karst Water** building up from beneath, carving out huge domes by its force.

Dome Hall and the **Giant Waterfall** are found within these caves.

Lake Hamor is fun for fishing, pedal boating or simply relaxing - and why not?

Lillafüred Narrow-gauge Railway - a fun way to travel from **Miskolc** to **Garadna.**

Married couples see this journey as a symbolic tribute to their own lives together.

Lillafüred Cable Car - good for viewing the surrounding scenery.

Aggtelek National Park - Karst Caves.
There are an amazing **712 Karst Caves** within this area,
shared between **Slovakia** and **Hungary.**
For us to mention them all here would take some doing
but we will tell you about a few of our favourites:
The colours, contours, formations and simply the
vastness of them is fantasmagorical.
A tour led by a guide speaking your own language is the
very best way to enjoy these caves.
Be prepared for a lot of walking.
Bring a sweater in summer as it will feel colder inside
but in winter, warmer.
All of these cave trips can be organised by the **Aggtelek
National Park Staff.**

Baradla is Europe's largest stalactite cave.
There are no less than three entrances and I
recommend you enter the cave from all three.
It is known as the **Baradla-Domica Cave Complex** and
is shared by both countries.

Meteor Cave in Bódvaszilas - For fit adults only.
A 2-4 hours long extreme route without any established
path, with a few ladders thrown in for good measure.
Ending within an enormous decorated hall.

Béke Cave is a wet walk, through water, which is
sometimes waist deep but does not involve any
climbing.

While you're up here on the border, nip over to visit **Domica Cave** on the **Slovak** side, it's only ten minutes in the car and both countries are in Schengen.
You will barely notice the border crossing.
Inside **Domica** take a boat ride on **Styx Creek.**
Yes, really - a boat ride underground on a lake!!!!!

Also to be found in **Aggtelek National Park:**
Hazel, forest and edible dormice and, on a larger scale - European badger, wild boar, roe deer and red deer, plus wildcat and wolf.

The U.K.

Non E.U. member
Non Schengen member
Very friendly towards tourists.

Do not forget to drive on the left hand side of the road and to be polite, despite the urge to become otherwise.

When touring the **U.K.** it is worth purchasing a **National Trust** and **English Heritage Membership Card.**
These will give free admittance to many country houses, estates and historical places of interest in all four of the **U.K. Countries,** which could prove to be very expensive to visit otherwise.

In addition to the above, **Wales** also offers a **Cadw Card** which allows free admittance to **Cadw Properties** and other sites in **Wales.**

There is also a **Scottish Heritage Card** which can also be used at **National Trust Sites in England, Wales** and **Northern Ireland** and a **Historic Scotland App** is available which can be used at all **Heritage** sites.

In **Northern Ireland** the **OPW Card (office of public works)** offers similar discounts and free entry to government owned properties.

Confused?

It is probably best to decide which sites you are going to visit before making up your mind about which cards to purchase.

Some sites, such as many on **Hadrian's Wall** for example, will accept both **National Trust cards** and also **English Heritage Cards**.
They may be managed by both organisations.

A visit to only three or four sites using a free entry card will certainly pay for itself.

Currency:
The pound sterling is the unit of currency throughout the U.K.
This is subdivided into 100 pennies.

Scotland has its own bank notes which are not always accepted in shops in England, Wales or Northern Ireland but can be exchanged at any bank or post office.
One U.K. pound sterling is worth 1.16 Euros.
One U.K. pound sterling is also worth 1.30 U.S. Dollars.

Bargaining over a purchase is not normal practice in the **U.K.** but who knows?
You may pick up a bargain if you try.

It is rare that a citizen of the **U.K.** will have fluency in any other language than their own but you may be surprised.
Some simple French may be offered.

Where language is a barrier, prepare to be shouted at very loudly as this tends to be the fallback mode of communication with foreigners by the 'Brits'. (Even visiting Americans and other English speaking citizens are likely to receive this treatment).

You may experience some thick, hard to interpret, English accents and dialects in various parts of the kingdom.

Be prepared to repeat your questions slowly and to ask for a reply several times.
If in doubt, simply shrug your shoulders and try again elsewhere.

England:

The south and south east of the country, particularly **London**, tends to be quite expensive compared to other European destinations.

If it is unavoidable to visit **London** I would suggest you buy a multiple ticket from the **Madame Tussauds Web Site** which will give entry to various sites managed by that group.

There are also various discounts and free travel cards available from **British Rail:**
The **London Oyster Card** is one of these.

In England, during the summer months, it is possible to experience an **English Civil War Battle Reenactment** at many of the sites that commemorate that war.
If you are able to, I would thoroughly recommend obtaining entry to one or two of these all day events. Information can be viewed here:
https://ecws.org.uk
And here:
https://earlofmanchesters.co.uk/the-battle-of-edgehill
And here:
https://www.bosworthbattlefield.org.uk

The latter - a two day event, would be on top of my to do list.

At the heart of England is the spring and summer fete.

These can be experienced in almost every town, village and hamlet.
You will see signs posted advertising these events as you travel.

Places of interest:

Lots of castles, everywhere.

Anywhere around the coast will provide beautiful scenery, and a variety of different interests and activities.

London:
The Capital City.
The capital city is famed for its very many historical sites.
During the previous 100 years, up until the mid 1960's, these could be enjoyed easily and pleasantly, however, greed and mass tourism has removed much of the enjoyment and grandeur of these sites.
Having said that, I would thoroughly recommend the **Horrible History's Terrible Trip** on the **Thames Tour**.
A great thing about **London** is that there are over 25 extremely interesting **Museums** and all of them are **Free!**
The majority of the very famous **Art Galleries** are also **Free!**
Whilst in London, one particular tradition that is worth experiencing is to take tea at **The Ritz Hotel**.
You will need to book well in advance for this treat.

Buckingham Palace - The home of the **Royal Family.**
Don't miss **Trafalgar Square** and **Piccadilly Circus.**

'Up North':

Northumberland:

Kielder Forest:
One of **England's** many fantastic national parks.
Miles and miles of forest, lakes, streams and waterfalls.
Excellent for long walks, bird watching, relaxing and
thinking.

Berwick - upon - Tweed:
The most northern town in England.
Has been regularly taken hostage by both **England** and
Scotand through the centuries.
Taking sides with each according to its own advantage.
A fascinating and pretty harbour town.

Lindisfarne /Holy island:
Managed by **English Heritage:**
Known for its mediaeval priory, sacked by Vikings.
The birthplace of the **Lindisfarne Gospels.**
An excellent day out and a must visit.

Seahouses - The original **'Kipper'** comes from here.

Hadrians Wall:
Built on the Roman border between **England** and
Scotland.

Running between **Newcastle** on the east coast and **Carlisle** in the west - **Rome's** final frontier.
Built in order to keep the Scottish hoards from raiding the farms and communities of England.
It's possible to walk along the total length of the wall in around 8 days. - Strong boots required.
There are many stopping places along the wall but six of the best, (as my headmaster was often heard to say), are from east to west:
Segedunum
Corbridge Roman Town
Chesters Roman Fort
Housesteads Roman Fort (my favourite).
Vindolanda Roman Fort
Birdoswald Roman Fort
More information on these can be found on their individual websites and also on both the National trust and English Heritage websites.

Cumberland, Lancashire and Westmorland:

The Lake District:
A vast area of lakes and woodland, hills and mountains.
Red squirrels, an endangered species in the U.K. can be seen here, scampering and foraging around.
Sheep, horses and cattle roam wild on the hills.
Famous for being the home of **Beatrix Potter** the world famous children's author.
A wonderful exhibition and tribute to her life can be found at **Bowness-on-Windermere.**

Hill Top, her home, is managed by the **National Trust** Near **Sawrey, Hawkeshead.**

The poets **William Wordsworth, Samuel Coleridge, Thomas de Quincey** and **John Ruskin** all lived in this area at various times and their lives can be explored by visiting where they lived and worked.

The homes of **William and Dorothy Wordsworth** can be visited at **Grasmere** and **Cockermouth.**

At **Ambleside** there is a very strange house built on a bridge - **The Bridge House.**

You are sure to be offered **Kendal Mint Cake**, a local sweet delicacy, at some point during your visit.

There are **tin, slate and lead mines** to be discovered, **Roman sites** to be uncovered and much more besides. Water sports and boat rides across the lakes. The mountains are widely climbed and walked and detailed maps and routes can be followed.

Scafell Pike, the highest mountain in England is to be found here, also **Helvellyn, Skiddaw** and **Great End.**

Yorkshire:
The South and **The North Yorkshire Moors:**

These are both such vast areas that to isolate a few places as being unique would be impossible. Anywhere upon these moors is an experience not to be missed.

North Yorkshire Moors:

To experience just a small area go to the very pretty town of **Pickering** and take a **Steam Train** to **Whitby.**
Stop off at **Goathland Station** along the route.
Visit **Robin Hoods Bay.**
Take a drive from **Kirkbymoorside** to **Castleton** and on to **Scaling Dam** via **Blakey Ridge** or **Rosedale Abbey,**

South Yorkshire Moors:

From **Harrogate** in the South, a town well worth spending a day at, to **Ravenstonedale,** which is actually in **Cumbria,** this too is a vast area to detail.
But we will try.

The Wensleydale Cheese Factory in **Hawes** may be a good place to begin.
There are some amazing walks to enjoy and waterfalls to wander at.

Aysgarth Falls is such a one.
Park at the restaurant for a walk down the short hill.
There are actually several immense falls which continue along the **River Ure** for some way.

Hardraw Force is another good one.
The Ingleton Waterfalls Trail will get you a good night's sleep.

Cautley Spout and **Cauldron Falls** too are well worth investigating.

Hawes is a market town and you won't want to miss the very busy weekly **Cattle and Sheep Market.**
There is a huge **Museum** in **Hawes** in the library building by the old railway station.

York:
Visit the **Jorvik Viking Museum**.
Walk the **City Walls**
Explore The new **Van Gogh Experience**
Spend a half day at **The National Railway Museum**
Do Not Miss - **The Castle Museum** (my favourite)
Clifford's Tower - A fascinating history and sad story of a massacre of Jews and their families.
York's Chocolate Story - Yummy!
Richard 111 Museum
Take **A Guided Bus Tour.**
Very worthwhile, restful and educational too!
Simply hop on where you like and hop off again, repeat.
Walk through **The Shambles -** unmissable!
The **Park And Ride Services** on the outskirts of **York** will save you a fortune in parking fees.
Jump on a bus and find your way around town on foot or on a **Tour Bus**.
Street Theatre is often to be discovered on the streets here which can be very pleasant and also professional too.
Don't forget to donate cash to these very hard working artists.

The East:

Norfolk:
Lots of very pretty beaches.
Plenty of opportunities to eat crab and other sea foods on the coast.
Famed for **'The Norfolk Broads'** an area of wetland.
Very picturesque villages with rivers and lakes. Very open flat area.

Sandringham Castle:
The country estate of Charles 111, the King of England.
It is possible to tour this estate but booking in advance is advised as it gets very busy.

Norwich is a town worth stopping off at.
There is an excellent **Castle, An Old Prison** and **A Museum.**

Suffolk:
Framlingham Castle is a good historical site.

Suton Hoo - Is brilliant.
A relatively recent discovery of a buried **Viking Ship** together with a hoard of viking goods.
It can be found on the strategically placed bend of the **River Deben.**

Cambridge:
A typical busy university town.

Some great buildings and monuments to explore.
An excellent public park where cattle still roam freely.
On the river **Cam** there are lots of opportunities to try your hand at punting.
Spanning the river there is a **Bridge of Sighs**, an imitation of the **Venetian** bridge of the same name.
The Fitzwilliam Museum is worth a good day's exploration.
King's College and **King's College Chapel** will be near the top of your places to visit list.
See also '**The Backs'** for picture postcard scenery - an area where the backs of several colleges meet in an area of open land alongside and over the river.
Cambridge University Botanic Gardens.
There are also at least **three theatres** and no less than **Two Swimming Pools.**
The shopping centre is quite something if you enjoy shopping and **Street Theatre** is often a feature here.

Essex:

Colchester:
Named **Camulodunum** by the Romans.
The very first **Roman Town** and the first capital town of England.
A fascinating history.
Tour **Colchester Castle** and the excellent **Museum** In **Castle Park.**

The Midlands:

Nottinghamshire:
The home of coal mining and silk weaving.

Near **Mansfield - Sherwood Forest.**
The haunt of **Robin Hood** and his **Merry Men.**
Also the site of **'The Great Oak'.**
Many trails and walks are available through this glorious woodland.

Newstead Abbey - Home of **Lord Byron.**

Nottingham Castle:
Famed for being the headquarters of the **Sheriff of Nottingham.**
Nottingham is also famous for its silk weaving and for the coal mining heritage.
Visit **Nottingham Museum** for great insights into its past.

Derbyshire:

The Peak District:
Rolling hills and dales, roaming sheep and cattle.
If you time your visit well, during May to September **Well Dressings** can be seen in most villages in the **Peak District.**
Chatsworth House - You really need two days for a good tour of **Chatsworth House and Gardens.**
Hear the story of **Deborah Mitford.** Worth every penny.
Home to the **Devonshire Family** for over five centuries and still inhabited by them today.

There is a strong relationship with **Hardwick Hall,** close by, which was built for '**Bess' of Hardwick** who also bought **Chatsworth House.**

Take the walk along the river at **Dovedale,** which is a wonderful walk, taking approximately two hours from '**Stepping Stones'** to **Milldale.**
Monsal Dale is another great day out.
At **Bakewell** sample the traditional **Bakewell Tart.**
There is a wonderful trail along an old railway line at **Tissington** which can be walked or taken easily by hiring a cycle at the trail's beginning.
The spa town of **Buxton** is not to be missed.
Explore the **Caves** at the **Blue John Mine** in **Matlock.**

Worcestershire:

Worcester Cathedral is well worth a visit - **King John, Prince Arthur and Prime Minister Stanley Baldwin** all have their tombs here.

Warwickshire:

Warwick Castle - The home of 'the kingmaker' **Richard Neville -** very influential during the English civil war.
Don't fail to visit the infamous **Dungeons** (not suitable for very young children).
There are often **Jousting Tournaments** and **Knights Revelries** during the summer months.

Coughton Court - Catholic home of **Guy Fawkes.**

Stratford Upon Avon - Home of **William Shakespeare.**

Buckinghamshire:

Stowe - Stowe Gardens (National Trust).
Excellent Gardens filled with follies and lakes, water features etc. Designed by **Capability Brown.**
Also the site of **Stowe Public School** where **King Rainier of Monaco,** who married the beautiful **Grace Kelly,** studied in 1935.
Billionaire business magnate **Richard Branson** also studied at **Stowe.**
His headmaster, Richard Drayton, told him that he would either become a millionaire or end up in prison.
Christopher Robin, the son of **A.A. Milne** also studied here but sadly was badly bullied and didn't enjoy it one bit.

'Down South':

Oxfordshire:

Blenheim Palace - The childhood home of wartime Prime Minister and M.P. **Winston Churchill.**

The Cotswolds:

An area of beauty that flows from **Warwickshire** through **Gloucestershire** and down as far as **Bath** in **Somerset.**

Note the brown, ironstone built houses and thatched cottages.

The old Roman road called **The Fosse Way,** which is the **A429,** will feature strongly in your travels in this area.

The Fosse Way was built by the Romans in order to connect **Exeter,** in the south west, with **Lincoln** in the north east.

Climb the tower at **Broadway.**

Visit the market town of **Moreton in the Marsh**, **Bourton on the Water** and **Chipping Campden, Chipping Norton** and **Stow on the Wold** for' **Olde Worlde'** charm - loads and loads of gift and antique shops.

Explore the Roman town of **Cirencester** and the lakes at **South Cerney.**

Berkshire:

Windsor:
Windsor Palace.
The occasional home of **The Royal Family.**

The Forest of Dean:

On the border with **Wales.**
Wild boar can often be seen, and their journeys noticed by the tracks left along the grass verges and through the woodland.

Recently introduced to the area, they are a mixed blessing for the local inhabitants.

There are also an abundance of deer, badgers and foxes, not to mention a vast array of birdlife including many birds of prey.

Here there are also amazing **Mines** to be burrowed in and **Peaks** to be climbed.

Look out for references to **Offa's Dyke** and **King Offa**. This **'Dyke'** passes through no less than eight counties on the border between **Wales** and **England**.

It can be seen at its start in **Chepstow** and also at **Lydney.**

King Offa was the ancient **King of Mercia.**

The **Dyke** was built in order to inhibit the **Welsh** invaders.

There is a ditch on the **Welsh** side.

The centre to begin a tour of this area would be **Symonds Yat,** on the **River Wye**, where **Peregrine Falcons** can be seen nesting.

Mallards Pike is also a good place for hiking and **Cannop Ponds.**

Do not miss - **The Forest of Dean Sculpture Trail -** Epic!

See **The Old Docks** at **Lydney Harbour** - once a thriving Port.

And take a **Steam Train Ride** right through the heart of the forest from **Norchard** to **Parkend**

Bristol:
A busy port town.

An excellent place to understand the history of England from the perspective of new initiatives.

Brunel's S.S. Great Britain was built here.

Banksy was born here.

John Cabot left here to discover North America.

John Wesley preached here for four years.

His old rooms and place of meeting are well worth visiting to get an idea of his situation.

Take a look at and drive over **Clifton Suspension Bridge -** an amazing feat of engineering - Don't look down!

Visit **Bristol Museum** and **Art Gallery.**

There is a huge, enormous, modern, covered, shopping mall - where you might well get lost and never seen again - **Cabot Circus** is its name but being **Bristol** you can't just have one shopping mall so you will also have to try **Cribbs Causeway** in order to compare the two.

Bath:

A very well preserved Romanised town sitting at the base of a huge hill.

Popularised by the Edwardians who left their mark in the architecture

Queen Boudicea was brought here to arrange a 'truce' with **Rome.**

There are some very interesting **Roman Baths.**

The town is one of the best in England.

Quite inexplicably relaxing, bearing in mind it is a tourist hot spot.

There are far too many **Museums** and **Art Galleries** to list here but you can almost pick your own depending upon your interests.

Bath's Abbey Tower is worth climbing just to get a view of the town.

You have a choice to make as to whether you come down on the side of the **Bath Bun,** a sweet roll sprinkled with fruit and crushed sugar, or the **Sally Lunn Bun,** part bun, part bread, a bit like a brioche but not really. Both are specialities here - spoilt for choice. Can't decide? Then try them both again.

The 'West Country':

Somerset:

Glastonbury:
Well known now for its summer concert.
Glastonbury Abbey is quite an amazing architectural experience.

Stonehenge: (National Trust and English Heritage) Is approximately 40 miles from **Glastonbury.** The site was once bought at auction by **Cecil Chubb** who went to the auction to buy chairs. When he gave it to the nation he insisted that no more than one shilling (5p) should be charged admittance and that locals would be able to visit freely.

In my opinion a better experience can be achieved by visiting **Avebury** (National Trust and English Heritage), a short drive down the road, with far more to see.

Cheddar:
Cheddar Gorge and **Caves.**
Cheddar Cheese.

Wells:
Wells Cathedral.
Wookey Hole Caves - In my opinion the best caves in the U.K.

Devon:

The home of **Devon Cream Tea's -** scones, strawberry jam and lots of thick cream.
Miles of **Sandy Beaches.**
Coastal towns and villages with great beaches**:**

Dunster Castle and Watermill is a good visit.

Minehead:
Great beach, a superb promenade and Butlins holiday camp.

Lynton and Lynmouth:
Travel up the **Cliff Railway.**
This was once the site of a devastating flood that left the two towns in tatters.

Combe Martin:
Great secluded beach

Ilfracombe:
Take a boat **Mackerel Fishing** and don't miss watching them make fudge in the famous **Fudge Shop** on the pier!

Woolacombe - Great for surfers

Saunton Sands:
Wonderfully sheltered and less windy than **Woolacombe**.
Good for rock pools.

Westward Ho!:
Named after Charles Kingsley's novel of the same name.
This is the only place name in the U.K. with an exclamation mark after it.

Spend some days (not nights) on **Exmoor** to get the feel of **Devon's** wild side.

Exmoor:
Ponies roam wild as do sheep and cattle and, it is rumoured, the odd large wild cat.
Puma's and other wildcats are believed to have been released into this environment during the government's animal regulations of the 1960's but are rarely to be seen.

Widdecombe-on-the-moor:
Is a good stop - watch out for Tom Pearse and his grey mare, not to mention, Bill Brewer, Jan Stewer, Peter Gurney, Peter Day, Daniel Whiddon, Harry Hawk and Old Uncle Tom Cobleigh.

Dartmoor:
Is idyllic and a great place to build dams and splash around in the rivers and streams.

Climb **Combestone Tor** for the breathtaking scenery. Watch out for the renowned top security prison on **Dartmoor,** on the road between **Rundlestone** and **Princetown -** Try not to pick up hitchhikers from this area.

There is a **Stone Circle** at **Brisworthy.**
Buckfast Abbey on the eastern edge is a tremendous day out - don't forget to sample the **'Fortified' Wine'.**

Devons South Coast:

Torquay:
A typical seaside town - one of my favourites.
For beauty and privacy go to **Mattiscombe Sands** and wander along, through **Lannacombe Beach**, to **East Prawl.**

At **East Portlemouth** you can catch a **Ferry** over to **Salcombe.**

Plymouth Historical Docks are well worth exploring.

Cornwall:
The Jurassic Coast:

Can be full of 'pesky tourists'.
Best visited out of season - early Spring or Autumn.
Dramatic coastline.
Rocky beaches, some sand.

Interestingly, it was probably to **Cornwall**, *or possibly western Spain,* that the boat was headed, that **Jonah** boarded when running away.
Cornwall was one of the furthest points west in those days and was a favourite of traders who collected the prized **Tin** to sell to the east.
There were only two small areas in the west where it could be obtained, making **Cornwall** extremely popular.

Cornwall is the home of **Poldark, Tin and Lead Mines** and tales of **Pirates**.
Daphne Du Maurier, wrote a book about cornish smugglers and life in the late 1700's - A tale of ship wreckers based around an old coaching Inn called **Jamaica Inn,** which is on the A30 at **Bolventor, Launceston.**
My Cousin Rachel is another one that you may enjoy reading whilst soaking up the ambience.

Whilst in **Cornwall** you may be forced to eat **Cornish Pasties.**

Do not attempt to resist, but be choosy.
Some are not as wonderful as others.
Do not go for the mass produced nonsense.
Look for an authentic **Cornish Pasty,** preferably freshly made on site or, even better, home made.
The big ones are best but you've got to be really hungry to survive the ordeal.

Dartmoor:
Lots of ponies, cattle and sheep roaming wild on the moors.
These animals look so cool and sweet and cuddly but please don't attempt to feed them or, in fact, cuddle them.
They can be quite defensive and a kick from a horse or pony is not pleasant.

These are not in truth wild animals but left throughout the year to fend for themselves and are gathered up on certain dates in order to sell them on.
They are strong, hardy animals and quite valuable.

Dartmoor is great for hiking over.
Always let someone know where you are heading for, and what time you expect to arrive.
Many people are lost on the moor each year.
There is rarely a mobile phone reception to call for assistance and fog can descend very quickly, disorientating even the wisest hiker.

The coastal towns and villages are very popular during the summer.

St Ives:

'As I was going to St Ives, I met a man with seven wives........'

A beautiful coastal resort, but watch out for the kamikazee, man killing, seagulls - Guard your chips with your life.

Penzance - Made famous by **Gilbert and Sullivan -** *'The Pirates of Penzance'.*

Looe - Stunning!

Polperro - Where there be real pirates!

Fowey - A wonderful coast and home to **Daphne Du Maurier.**

Padstow:

An independent fishing harbour.

Sadly spoiled by '**Rick Stein world'.**

Very commercialised now, but try to imagine what it was like 60 years ago!

Where the two pubs were filled only with local fishermen, sea shanties and French smugglers and not a chip shop, gift shop, art centre or restaurant within 20 miles.

Tintagel:

Where **Merlin**, of **King Arthur** legend, has his castle .

Lizard - A peninsular - terrific and few tourists!

Lands End:
The most southerly point in the U.K.
We can go no further.
The next stop due west is the U.S.A.

The Eden Project:
An excellent day out!
A 'Not to be missed' day!!!!!!
Several exclamation marks are required to express how good this is.
Buy tickets online well in advance.
Best to go 'out of season' to avoid the crowds - winter is fine as it's mostly indoors.

The Scilly Isles:

A part of the historic **County of Cornwall.**
Around 140 islands make up the archipelago that is the
Scilly Islands but only five are inhabited:

There are useful **Island Hopping Boats** available.
Also **Bike Hire** to make it easy to get around.
There are some cute and cuddly **Seals** to spy on, lots of
sea adventures to be had plus good bird watching too!

St Mary's:
Bant's Carn Burial Chamber and **Halangy Down
Ancient Village.**
Prime minister **Harold Wilson's** holiday home is here.
Try your skill at **Wine Tasting - Holy Vale Vineyard.**
There's a good walk to **Innisidgen Lower** and **Upper
Burial Chambers.**
If you are ready to cool off - visit the **Normandy
Swimming Pool,** open all year.

Tresco:
Abbey Garden is so peaceful and unique in all the
world.
Cromwell's Castle (English Heritage) - nestling
between **Bryher** and **Tresco** is one of the few surviving
Cromwellian Fortifications in Britain.

St Martin's:
Vineyard and Winery, Visitor Centre. - good job we're
not driving 'eh?

Interested in ceramics? **'Throw a Pot'** here.

St Agnes:
Tranquillity is what you will find here in bucketloads.
The island can be walked over in a day.
At **Gugh** during low tide there is **Bronze Age, Obadiah's Barrow,**

Bryher:
The perfect place for eating **Shellfish** of every description.
The very, very last stop before the American coast!
Great for **Fishing** and **Beaching.**
Plenty of **Artists Studios** here to wander through.
Don't miss the amazing **Phone Box Mini-Museum**

The Channel Islands:

Although not strictly a part of the U.K.
They are dependent territories of the British Crown, as successor to the Dukes of Normandy.
Situated just off the French coast of **Brittany.**
These Islands, set adrift from mainland U.K., suffered greatly during the second world war when they became occupied territory.
There are many reminders of this conflict scattered around the islands.

Guernsey:

A Discovery Pass will cost just £22.00 and is valid for 12 months.
It allows an adult holder seasonal entry to **Castle Cornet, Guernsey Museum, Fort Grey** and the **German Naval Signals Headquarters,** - all accompanying children under 18 years go free.

I might suggest that you watch the film '**The Guernsey Literary and Potato Peel Pie Society',** to get a feel of **Guernsey** during the 2nd world war.

St. Peters Port:
The Capital Town.
A great little harbour and beach.
There are **History** and **Military Museums** housed within the **Harbour Fortifications.**

The author of **Les Miserables', Victor Hugo,** once lived here in **Hauteville House.**

Castle Cornet is a gem of a Castle - Hold your hands over your ears at noon when the Cannons fire!

Les Niaux Water Mill.

German Occupation Museum.

Vazon Bay Beach is exceptional.

Shingle Bank Nature Reserve. - Wonderful opportunities for sea life and birds.

Close by - **St. Saviour Nature Reservoir.**

Jersey:

Gerald Durrell's one time home.

Here he founded **The Durrell Wildlife Conservation Trust** and the **Jersey Zoo.**

St Helier - Jersey's capital town.

The place to do some shopping.

By special dispensation of the U.K. government - **No V.A.T.** to be paid here, so grab some well discounted goodies!

Central Market is the place to browse away the day.

Elizabeth Castle is a fun visit - set on a causeway so can only be reached at low tide.

The walk takes about 15 minutes.

If you miss the tide.......

Mont Orgueil Castle - Lots of historical references here and superb views across to **Normandy** in **France!**

St Brelade's Bay - Jersey's prettiest beach.

La Rocque Harbour - Less crowded - A sandy beach too - excellent for crabbing and collecting winkles.

Les Mielles Nature Reserve - Peace and tranquillity - so much to see here.

Right on the beaches and sunsets to die for.

Pallot Steam Museum - spend a few hours soaking yourselves in nostalgia.

Some amazing steam vehicles here.

Alderney:

3 Miles long and just about 1.5 miles wide.

No crowds and no queues!

St Anne is at the centre of the Island.

Braye Beach is one of the most popular beaches and **Platte Saline** is not far behind.

Fort Clonque and '**The Guns**' - **Gun Emplacements -** Two good sites to visit.

Also **Fort Quesnard** on the opposite end of the Island

Sark:

Is a car free island.

There are great ways to get around though, such as on horseback or pony and trap, or by bike.

Walking is fine as well as the Island is only 3.5 miles x 1.5 miles.

There are around 500 inhabitants on **Sark.**

The language of **Sark** is **Sercquiais,** also known as **Sarkese** or **Sark-French (Lé Sèrtchais).**

It is a Norman language.

Only 4 people can speak it.

The Window in the Rock - A geological formation.
Watch out for the drop!!
La Seigneurie - An estate built during the 1500's upon a 6th century monastery.
Very sedate and luxurious.
Sark Museum - Very interesting.
Caragh Chocolates - With free cake!!!

Hern:

2,183m long and under 873m wide.
No vehicles are allowed on this Island also.
It is possible to walk from **The Harbour** to **Rosaire Steps** in about seven minutes.
The walk from **The Harbour** to **Shell Beach** takes about 20 minutes and from **The Harbour to Belvoir Bay** takes about 15 minutes.
There is a population of 65 who live on the Island.
Shell Beach is a big attraction with a plethora of fantastic shells.
Here you can see seals, puffins and go dolphin-spotting.
A walk around **Hern Garden** is well worth the time as well.

Jethou:

Home to **Smugglers** and **Pirates** in days gone by.
Perfect silence and peace today.
The summit was once home to a gallows, where **Pirates** would be hanged.

262

Brecqhou (Brechou):

David and Frederick Barclay, twins, were the only two inhabitants on the island until David died in 2021.
Their home is something to see.
A mock gothic affair with thick granite walls, two swimming pools and a helicopter pad.

Wales:

Mountains and valleys. Slate and coal mines.
Lakes and Rivers.
Slate roofed cottages and ruined chapels.
Beautiful rugged coastline.

There are lots and lots of superb **Castles** in Wales,
mostly built for **Edward 1** In his bid to conquer that part
of the U.K. but also some surprises.

The Welsh are quite keen on the revival of their own
national language.
There are many centres where the language can be
studied and efforts are being made to remove all traces
of the English language where possible.

North Wales:

Anglesey:
An area of outstanding natural beauty.
Great place to find red squirrels still.
There are deterrents to stop the grey ones galloping
over the **Britannia Bridge.**
The Menai Suspension Bridge and **The Britannia
Bridge** straddle **The Menai Strait** from **Bangor** to **The
Isle of Anglesey.**
A fantastic feat of engineering.

Being virtually cut off from the mainland, **Anglesey** is a wealth of nature and a great place to escape the hustle and bustle.

Baumauris Castle - A must not miss day out. - Well worth every penny.

The Snowdonia National Park. (Eryn National Park).
823 square miles of beauty.

Snowdon:
The highest mountain in **Wales** and second highest in the U.K.
Put on your strong boots for a good walk up its slopes, which will take you upwards of four hours, or take an amazing ride up and down again in the train.

Conwy Castle:
Built in the 13th Century For Edward 1
Along with **Caernarvon Castle** and **Beaumaris Castle** on **Anglesey.**
All three are an excellent visit and well worth the entrance fee.
The **Suspension Bridge** at **Conwy** is also a marvellous piece of engineering.

Caernarfon Castle:
An unforgettable visit.
You will need at least one whole day here and still not see everything.
One of the greatest castles built during the Middle ages.
Built for Edward 1.

Fantastic historical site and museum.

At **Porthmadog** jump on to **The Welsh Highland Heritage Railway.**
To take an amazing, unforgettable journey on a steam train, up into the mountains, along **The Ffestiniog Railway line,** all the way to the **Welsh Slate Mines** at **Blaenau Ffestiniog.**
Wander around the **Slate Mines** and do some shopping before returning to the wonderful beach and harbour at **Porthmadog.**
You can also take the **Welsh Highland Railway Steam train** from **Caernarfon,** which runs for 25 miles, past the foot of **Snowdon** and the picture postcard village of **Beddgelert,** then through the stunning **Aberglaslyn Pass** and on to **Porthmadog.**
Whilst at Blaenau Ffestiniog don't miss the opportunity to visit the majestic **Cwmorthin Waterfall** and **Cwmorthin Lake.**

The coastline around **Tywyn** and **Aberdovey** is astounding - first class.

Tal-y-llyn Lake, also known as **Talyllyn Lake** and **Llyn Myngul.**
Unbeatable in terms of tranquillity and beauty.
Take a swim in the lake when the weather allows but this area is superb at any time of year.

A drive around **Bala Lake** will get your eyes popping, for the scenery is momentous!

Sit, with a bag of chips, to view the evening scene as birds dip and dive in the sunset.

Elan Valley - You will need to spend a week here to fully appreciate the wonder of the valleys and heights.
Visit the **Elan Dam** and walk around some of the lakes.
Enjoy the woodland.

Brecon Beacons - From **Llandovery Castle** to the old mining town of **Abergavenny.**
From **Hay on Wye**, just within the English border, to **Castell Carreg Cennen.**
There's so much to experience.
Take a drive from **Sennybridge** to **Abercraf** to experience the bleak moorland of the **Beacons.**

Pembroke:

Pembroke Castle:
Birthplace of the first Tudor, **Henry V11** in 1457. Britain's only Welsh King.
(Information added by Roselle Francis, aged 12, on 26th July 2023).
The largest privately-owned castle in Wales.
The castle is also noteworthy for being Britain's only castle built over a natural cave, known as **The Wogan**, which has been inhabited since **The Prehistoric Era.**
Oliver Cromwell ordered the castle to be destroyed and encouraged the villagers to take pieces of it home with them.
It has since been restored thanks to various owners.

The Coast:
Visit any and every single one of the villages on the coast of **Pembrokeshire** and you will not be disappointed with any of them.

Wales has an abundance of picturesque and fascinating villages - enough to keep anyone filled with enjoyment and surprise for many years.

Carmarthenshire:

Tenby - One of my favourite beaches.
Pendine Sands, in the midst of a truly amazing coast, is where **Sir Malcolm Campbell** raced his very famous **Sunbeam Racing Car.**

Gower Peninsular:

Loughor:
The Loughor River Estuary.
Loughor Castle was built by **Henry de Beaumont,** the **Earl of Warwick** in 1106 and has a fascinating history. Once given to **King John** and then taken by **Prince Llywelyn the Great.**
Battles between the **English Kings** and **Wales** was a common scene around this area for over one hundred years.
It was in the town of **Loughor** that revival broke out in 1904 and quickly spread throughout **Wales**, particularly into the **Isle of Anglesey** and into **England.**

Hundreds of thousands of people were brought into freedom, so much so that the entire shape and mood of both countries were changed.

The newspapers of that era were full of examples of miraculous changes in the lives of the worst criminals of the time.

Miracles appear to have been commonplace.

The Mumbles:

A very fine peninsular.

You will want to visit every one of the beaches here too. The worry of missing just one gem will be too hard to bear.

Excellent for Rock Pools, Crab Fishing, Catching Winkles, Bathing, Swimming, Fishing and Eating.

Cardiff:

Has a history reaching way back to Roman times and earlier.

Visit **Cardiff National Museum.**

It is a mine of entertainment and information and it's free!

There are a lot of **Museums** in Cardiff that will welcome and entertain for hours, if not days.

Cardiff Castle is an excellent day out.

Built during the 11th Century and commissioned by **William the Conqueror.**

The **Dr. Who Walking Tour** is a must-do experience.

Bute Park is a great place for children, picnic and a stroll around beautiful parklands.

At nearby **Creigiau** - visit **St. Fagans Open Air National Museum of History.**

It's very interactive and hours of fun.

Fforest Fawr:
Castell Coch - The Red Castle.

Built on the ruins of a **Norman Fort** during the 19th century.

A fairy tale castle with history.

This is a castle which is very different from others you may have visited.

There is a strong Gothic French influence here for good reason.

Scotland:

Whiskey. Highland Cattle and Kilts.
Haggis, Bagpipes, far away lonely islands, Lochs and
Mysterious Monsters.

Scotland is the place to go to **'Bag a Munro'.**

There are many mountains and lower hills in Scotland.

These are graded according to their heights above sea
level:
A Munro is a peak that is above 3000 feet.

There are many climbers who 'collect' **Munro's** by
climbing them one by one.
There are 282 **Munros** to collect.

In addition to **Munros,** there are also **Corbetts,
Grahams and Donalds.**
At one time there were also **Elsie's,** but alas, no longer.
You will enjoy discovering the difference in these as you
travel.

The isles of **Scotland t**ravel as far north as The **Faroe
Isles** which appear to be closer to **Iceland** or **Norway**
than the **U.K.**
Indeed many of the islands that surround mighty
Scotland were once the responsibility of these closer
civilisations as the Viking nations ruled supreme.

In truth, archaeologists are only recently discovering that the north of Scotland was once known, world wide as the centre of civilisation and was very wealthy, a leader in religious gatherings and culturally head and shoulders above the wider world.

In short, Scotland is steeped in history from its early neolithic days, evidence of which can be found everywhere, through to its Viking conquerors, the Roman wars and more recently the near 300 years of battles with England and the oppressors.
This aggression, desire for independence and reluctance to remain a part of the U.K. appears to continue today through its political ambitions.

The Orkneys:
Visit **Skara Brae** to fire your imagination and to set you searching for other close and related sites.
Then move on to **Maeshowe,** the **Ring of Brodgar** and the **Standing Stones of Stenness.**
Said to be influential in the building of **Stonehenge** in the south of England.
You will not be disappointed, no matter the weather.

John o' Groats:
The furthest point on the Scottish mainland, and worth a visit in order to gaze at the vast coldness of the North sea towards the **Northern Isles** of **Orkney and Shetland.**

There are few roads, many mountains and much beauty to explore in this **Highland Country.**

Travelling through these majestic mountains and valleys you may well spot your first **Wild Haggis.**
These shy, timid wee creatures roam wild up here in the north of the country, on the slopes that are less frequented.

An odd feature of these furry animals is that they have two legs on one side that are longer than the other side to enable them to balance on the precipitous gradient of the steeper hills.

You may find the Highland Scottish accent very interesting, almost a language apart from English.

On the west side we can visit **The Hebrides** and the **Small Islands -** each one is a gem and filled with its own beauty and specialist natural surroundings.

Kyle of Lochalsh is the place to find a bridge over to **The Isle of Skye.**
You have my permission to sing '**The Skye Boat Song**' at this point. -
'Sweet bonnie boat, like a bird on the wing,'.......

There are also plenty of other things to see and do here - **Castles** and **Hikes, Museums** and a great **Harbour.**

There are approximately **30,000 Lochs in Scotland,** each one more beautiful and picturesque than the last, so you will be sure to bump into a few on your travels around these areas.

From **Inverness** travel down to **Loch Ness.**
Keep your eyes peeled for the infamous and shy **Loch Ness Monster** or **'Nessie'** as she is affectionately known.
There is mention of an underground tunnel, leading out to the open sea from **Loch Ness** which could well be why few people have ever seen her.

From **Loch Ness** we must backtrack a little in order to travel through the **Cairngorms National Park** on our way to **Aberdeen -** Don't miss **Balmoral Castle -** beloved home of the **King's Grandmother** on the way through the **Cairngorms.**

We can then travel down the coast road to **Dundee** for tea and **cake.**
If you enjoy golf you will be sure to want to visit **St Andrews.**

Edinburgh will be next **- Edinburgh Castle.**
If you plan your timing right, arrive in August to catch **The Edinburgh Fringe!!**

And I hope you are allowing plenty of time to take in these fabulous historic towns.

Travel west to reach **Glasgow -** a new Scottish accent to fathom and another couple of days will be well spent here.

Turn north again to call in at **Loch Lomond -**
*'You take the high road and I'll take the low road, and I'll be in Scotland 'afore ye, but me and my true love will never meet again, on the bonny, bonny banks of **Loch Lomond'.***

Spend a good few days exploring **The Trossachs National Park.**

Then on up to **Glencoe -** You will remember the **Battle of Glencoe** from your history lessons?
The Scots refer to it as **'The Massacre of Glencoe'.**
*One dark, wintery night in February 1692, members of the resident **MacDonald Clan** were murdered, as they slept by troops of the **Clan Campbell.***
Operating under orders from the Government, thirty-eight men, women and children all perished.
The wounds are still very sore.

Ballachulish:
The Meeting of Three Waters also known as **Glencoe Falls.**
The location of **The Bridge of Death** and the **Gorge** of **Eternal Peril** in **"Monty Python and the Holy Grail."**
Such a scene of beauty and tremendous force is hard to describe until it is seen with your own eyes.
A perfect visual picture of Scotland at its best.

Fort William:
A climbers paradise!
Ben Nevis:
The highest mountain on the British isles.
Well worth the effort to climb.
Will take approximately 8 hours up and down if you are fit.

You may wish to turn west here to **Mallaig** in order to catch a ferry to **The Hebrides.**

The Hebrides:
Here the **Gaelic Language** can be heard, spoken quite widely.

The Isle of Lewis:
The furthest of the **Isles of Hebrides.**
Stornoway:
The largest town on **Lewis**.
Lews Castle is one of the main features of this Island.
The wildlife and particularly the sea birds are, of course, wonderful.
It was on **The Isle of Harris,** in the tiny hamlet of **Barvas,** that what is known as '**The Hebridean Revival**' broke out in 1949 and swept through the Islands.
Over **20,000 people** were brought into freedom during those days.
Many notable miracles were experienced during those days as can be today when the people of God are willing to live in faith.

Oban is a fine old Scottish town and you will enjoy eating **Venison** here or perhaps your first **Haggis?**

The Isle of Mull, The Mull of Kintyre, The Isle of Arran and Jura can all be reached by ferry from **Oban.**

The Hebrides too can be accessed from **Skye, Mallaig** or **Oban.**

Galloway Forest Park in '**The Lowlands'** is one of Scotland's southernmost **National Parks** and one of the best places to view **The Northern Lights.**
A mountainous and well forested Park.
As well as plenty of deer and wild goats you can see Black grouse, red squirrels, otters and nightjars here.

Northern Ireland:

Misty Mountains, Warm Pubs, Folk Songs and Irish Jigs.

St Patrick or **Padraig,** as he was known, is the patron saint of Ireland.

The title of *'saint'* is one that was manufactured by the Catholic religion.
The first mention of a *'saint'* being a person of higher notability was in 993.

In truth everyone who is born again of God is a saint.
The term simply means 'holy one'.
All of those who are joined to God are holy ones, there is no elite group who are holier than others.

It's strange to relate that Patrick was not of Irish stock at all but a slave who had been kidnapped from his family estate, possibly in **South Wales,** by marauding pirates.
He was then kept captive in Ireland for 12 years before escaping.

He was educated in what was then **Gaul** and later came back to Ireland to teach the natives about Jesus.
He was certainly a gifted man and filled with God's Spirit.

There were many who decided to become born again as a result of his efforts.

He was known to use the three-leafed shamrock in order to explain how God could be three in one - The Father, The Son and also Spirit.

Our route around Northern Ireland follows in an anticlockwise direction for no reason at all.

All of Ireland has a beauty that is unique to this ancient Island.

Before visiting any part of **Ireland,** whether **North** or **South,** read **Spike Milligan's Book - Puckoon.** It's hilarious reading and will set the scene for you.

Belfast:
Visit the **Renovated Dockyards** to tour the **R.M.S. Titanic Museum** at the old **Harland and Wolff Docks. The World's Leading Tourist Attraction!!**
Now hosting an **Underwater Cinema,** several fascinating **Museums** and often **Concerts** on the Slipways as well.
There are **5000 acres of Parkland** in Belfast. So there's never far to go for a peaceful stroll or a picnic.
St George's Market is a must visit with hundreds of stalls, representing **Belfast's Heritage,** from **Metal Work** to **Goat Meat, Sea Food and Soda Bread,** also - **Free Jazz Music** at the weekends.
The Botanical Gardens are excellent as is **Ulster Museum.**

Belfast Castle - The inspiration for **Jonathan Swift's Gulliver's Travels** is a must, which is sited in the exciting and exhilarating **Cave Hill Country Park.** Named after the five caves that are in the cliffs. Try your hand at **Orienteering** or almost any other outdoor activity here.
Only five minutes away from **Belfast Zoo.**

County Antrim:

The Coast of Glens and Outstanding Natural Beauty: The Gobbins to **Cushendale.**

There are around 107 mountains to explore in **Antrim.** One of the best and possibly highest is **Trostan Mountain.**

The Gobbins:
If you're after adventure and adrenaline take this around the cliffs rope walk - Amazing fun and great views too!

Larne:
A perfect base for exploring the glens and coastal route up to **Ballycastle.**
Carnfunnock Country Park might be your first stop off. Plenty to do here for the family.
An immense park offering **Gardens, Walking Trails, Golf, Orienteering,** an **Adventure Playground** and much more in the summer months.
There is also a caravan and camping site.

The Causeway Coastal Route and the **Nine Glens:**

Cushendall:
The very best base to explore the backdrop of mountains and the closest village to **Trostan Mountain.**

Cushendun:
A picture postcard harbour village with fishing boats, superb beaches and more **Caves** to explore!!

Ballycastle:
An ancient viking settlement.
Perfectly formed harbour from which a ferry to **Rathlin Island** can be taken.
Knocklayde Mountain can be explored from here too.

Rathlin Island:
Breathtakingly beautiful.
Home to many **Seals** and a multitude of **Puffins** and other sea birds.
It was once a part of a greater kingdom that included the **Mull of Kintyre,** now a part o**f Scotland.**
It is said to be the site of **Robert the Bruce's** encounter with the spider that changed the course of history in 1309.
The foot passenger ferry will take you there in 25 minutes, whilst the car ferry will take around 35 minutes.

Near **Ballintoy:**
Carrick-A-Rede Rope Bridge. (National Trust).

This perilous rope bridge connects the mainland with the tiny island of **Carrickarede.**
It spans 20 metres and is 30 metres above the rocks below.
It was first erected by salmon fishermen in 1755.

2 miles from **Bushmills Village - Giants Causeway:**
Over 40,000 basalt columns.

Portrush:
Excellent beach here and because of its location - great for surfers too!

The Barmouth, Castlerock Beach, Portstewart Strand.
A two mile stretch of glorious sand.
The dunes here are the tallest in Ireland.
Supposedly the birthplace of the **Irish Harp.**

Magilligan Point:
The tip of one of the largest sand dune systems in the British Isles.
A sparse and amazing **Nature Reserve.**
Watch out though because part of it is also a British Army firing range!

Binevenagh:
An Area of Outstanding Natural Beauty
Formed 60 million years ago.
The hill itself allows panoramic views over **Lough Foyle.**

Sperrins:
Sperrin Nature Reserve:
The Sperrin Mountains.
Teeming with wildlife, dramatic mountains, lakes and streams.
A walker's paradise and a climber's dream.

Kesh:
On the border with Ireland.
On the **River Kesh** and the banks of **Lower Lough Erne.**

Lower Lough Erne:
There is so much to see here - bring your binoculars!
A vast and picturesque Lough.
View **The Cliffs of Magho** - stunningly scenic!
Blackslee Waterfall is well worth the short walk - better in the rainy season.

Enniskillen:
The largest town in **County Fermanagh.**
Enniskillen Castle Museums are interesting as is **Castle Coole** although not really a castle but a **Manor House.**
Nevertheless it is one of The National Trust's best properties in Northern Ireland and well worth visiting.

Upper Lough Erne:
A glorious hidden treasure.
Great walking country and fishing too!
Superb for bird watching and just chilling out.

Hire out a boat for the day or even a week.

Belle Isle Estate, Castle & Cottages
Here at the north of the **Lough** you can **Rent a Castle!**
A real live **17th Century Castle** on a 470-acre estate
spread across 8 private islands.
Once owned by the **McManus Clan**, the present owner
is **The Duke of Abercorn.**

Oxford Island Nature Reserve:
On the banks of **The Lough Neagh.**
Excellent place to view and study wildlife.
Reed beds, open water, wildlife ponds, forests and
wildflower meadows.
There is a network of walking trails, bird watching hides,
the **Lough Neagh Discovery Centre, Kinnego Marina**
and the **Kinnego Bushcraft Centre.**
Plus they make an excellent cup of tea and a slice of
cake.

Lough Neagh:
This is not only the largest lake in all of **Ireland** but in all
of the **U.K**.
It spreads itself over 151 square miles.
What to do around this area?
Simply close your eyes and imagine….

Ring Of Gullion:
Mountain drives and hill walking, rock climbing, nature
rambles, photography, canoeing and cycling to horse
riding, bird watching, fishing and golf.

Slieve Gullion is the peak to climb and after that, relax and enjoy Ireland at its best.

There is another way to enjoy the peak, for the less agile - It is possible to drive around the route.

Start at the cafe in the Forest Park and head up the mountain. It is a one-way drive.

Children will love the **Slieve Gullion Adventure Park** and the **Red Squirrel Safari, Scenic Drive** there is also a **5000 Year Old Passage Tomb!**

To the South East of Newry:
Mountains of Mourne:

The Mountains o' Mourne
by Percy French (1902)

Oh, Mary, this London's a wonderful sight,
With people all working by day and by night.
Sure, they don't sow potatoes, nor barley, nor wheat,
But there's gangs of them digging for gold in the street.
At least when I asked them that's what I was told,
So I just took a hand at this digging for gold,
But for all that I found there I might as well be
Where the Mountains o' Mourne sweep down to the sea.

Made famous more recently by Don McLean. (1973)
Recently? Ha!

There are only twelve peaks to master here.
For a true taste of Ireland's beauty take the drive up the side of the mountains from **Hilltown**, and then back

down the otherside again to **Newcastle** - a wonderful beach.

A drive across from **Hilltown** to **Kilkeel** or **Glasdruman** will also melt your heart.

Visit **Silent Valley Mountain Park** and walk to the reservoir, stopping for a cup of tea and some cake on the way.

Tollymore Forest Park:

Explore the forest.

The site of many **Game of Thrones** scenes.

It will take around 5 hours to cover the whole park but take it slowly or make two or three days of it.

Castle Ward: (National trust).

Facing and on the edges of, **Strangford Lough.**

A gigantic property and immense grounds.

Lady Anne's grandfather was the nephew of the Duchess of York – wife of King James II and a first cousin of Queen Anne.

Strangford Lough:

A sea water lough.

In the midst of an area of outstanding beauty.

The site for many sea birds, waders and dibbers.

There are some good long walks to be had here, most of which are on good firm solid ground.

Royal Hillsborough Castle and Gardens:

This is an **Historical Royal Residence.**

Elizabeth II and the Duke of Edinburgh stayed in **Hillsborough Castle** during their visit to **Northern Ireland** as part of the Golden Jubilee tour of the United Kingdom in 2002.
A good day out and well worth the expensive fee to visit. Ask for a tour guide for more interesting information.

Which will bring our tour of **Northern Ireland** back to **Belfast.**
Just in time to catch the ferry home!

Gibraltar:

A British Overseas Territory

The Monkeys on **Gibraltar** are **Barbary Macaques** which would have originally come from the **Atlas Mountains** in **Morocco.**

How they arrived in **Gibraltar** sometime during the 1700's remains a mystery but they were encouraged to breed and are fed and looked after by the **British Government.**

There are 34 miles of hidden tunnels under the rock, some of which date back as far as the 1700's. Some of the caves may have been used by **Neanderthals.**

Places of interest:

Upper Rock Nature Reserve:
Covering around 40% of the total land mass which is Gibraltar, from where most of the territory can be seen as well as the **Costa Del Sol** below and **North Africa** in the distance.
It is possible to reach the summit by **Cable Car,** on foot or by hailing a local cab.

Great Siege Tunnels:
Also known as the **Upper Galleries,** are a series of tunnels inside the northern end of the Rock of Gibraltar.

They were dug out from the solid limestone by the British during the Great Siege of Gibraltar of the late 18th century when Spanish forces were determined to claim the rock as their own.
They also came in very useful during ww2 when defending them and the straits against German attack.

Mediterranean Steps:
One of the many treks around the **Nature Reserve.**
This one is mildly easy and should take approximately ninety minutes to keep you trim.
Dogs aren't allowed on this particular trek.
It is good for bird watching, forestry and wildlife.

St. Michael's Cave.
The name given to a network of **Caves** beneath **Gibraltar.**
It was once thought to be bottomless.
This **idea** gave birth to the story that the **Rock of Gibraltar** was linked to **Africa** by a subterranean passage under the **Strait of Gibraltar.**

Moorish Castle:
A range of fortifications and buildings on the hilltop.
It was in fact built by the **Marinid Dynasty** which is a rare find in these parts.
It is now one thousand years old.

Gibraltar Botanical Gardens:

The Alameda is a **Wildlife Conservation Park** with much more to see than plants, although these are a treat to wander around.

Admission is free.

Plants from all around the world.

Europa Point:

The southernmost point of Gibraltar.

Next stop **Morocco.**

There is also a **Lighthouse** here guiding navigation along the strait below.

The last time the strait opened up was around five million years ago and there were no humans around to watch it happen.

It must have been a spectacular event.

The Mediterranean had been land-locked for a very long time and had evaporated.

Then as a fissure developed where the **Strait of Gibraltar** is today, the Atlantic gushed in filling the Mediterranean basin in just one hundred years, with a huge ten thousand foot waterfall at the entrance to the strait.

Ireland:

Schengen rules apply.
90 day maximum stay in E.U. applies.

Ireland is a confirmed member of the European Union.

The currency, as in most member states, is the Euro.

Can be reached by car ferry from the U.K. and also from the French ports of Cherbourg and Roscoff.

The fastest route from the U.K. is from **Fishguard** in **Wales** to **Rosslare** in **County Wexford.**

You cannot visit Ireland without experiencing the warm pubs, where folk songs fill the evening and everyone appears to be a relative.

Ireland is an extremely friendly Island to be on - Once here, you will not want to leave.

Places of interest:

A good route to take from the ferry at **Rosslare** might be:

South to:

Waterford:
One of Ireland's oldest communities.

Visit the world famous glass factory.
Thousands of years of history. - Fascinating.

Cork:
A visitor could spend several days in and around Cork.
Beautiful countryside, coastline and wonderful people.

Blarney:
Blarney castle.

Skibbereen:
Historic Town.

Schull:
Take a boat ride around the coast or visit an island.
Colin the boatman will be pleased to take you out for the day whale and dolphin spotting.
Charming harbour and coast.

Killarney:
There are so many things to see and do here - Don't miss **The Ring of Kerry**!
You will never forget.
Torc Waterfall, Killarney National Park, and the **Meeting of the Waters.**
Rose Castle, Killarney Lakes, The Ladies View and much more besides.

From **The Head of the Gap of Dunloe** take the back road, through **The Gap of Dunloe,** to **Kate Kearney's Cottage.**

An amazing, unforgettable drive and a wonderful story to hear at **Kate Kearney's Cottage** too.

Dingle:
A drive around the **Dingle Peninsula** is a must with amazing views and fantastic castline.
At **Dingle** take time for a boat ride to visit and swim with **Fergy the Dolphin** who loves to play with visitors.

Tralee:
From **Tralee** take the back roads to
Tarbert where it is possible to board the **Shannon Car Ferry** over the mighty **Shannon River** to **Killimer.**

Limerick:
Famed for amusing poetry.

Ennis and **Galway** are well worth visiting for the atmosphere, pubs and nightlife as well as stocking up.

Lough Derg:
Very many spots to rest awhile and enjoy the tranquil waters and wildlife.

Kilkenny:
Medieval Castle worth spending some time in.
People who live in **Kilkenny** are often referred to as **'Cats'.**

Dublin:
The home of **'Molly Malone'.**

Molly, the fishmonger's daughter, was representative of many poor and starving children who sold their wares on **Dublin's** streets during the 17th century.

In Dublin's fair city
Where the girls are so pretty
I first set my eyes on sweet Molly Malone
As she wheeled her wheelbarrow
Through streets broad and narrow
Crying, "Cockles and mussels, alive, alive, oh!"
Alive, alive, oh
Alive, alive, oh
Crying, "Cockles and mussels, alive, alive, oh"

Sadly, poor Molly '*died of a fever',* as many others did.

Visit the famous **Guinness Factory.**
Take a 'free' pint at the top of the viewing tower.
Dublin Castle. Kilmainham Gaol.
Tucked away next to the castle is the **Chester Beatty Library Museum** - an amazing place to spend some time in and is absolutely **Free!**
The Book of Kells is housed in **Trinity College.**
While you're in college, pop into **The Library** and don't miss **'The Long Room'**. Over 300 years old, 213 feet long and houses 200,000 books.
Many fascinating museums, some relating to Ireland's turbulent past.
Modern shopping and business centres.
Busy and varied nightlife. Theatres, restaurants. Parks.

France:

Schengen rules apply.
90 day maximum stay in E.U. applies.

France is the largest country in the E.U.

It can be subdivided into eighteen administrative regions. Thirteen of which are within mainland france.

There are a few notable historic events that should be mentioned before we begin our tour.
The Hundred Years War with the English might be one.

It officially began on **May 24th 1337.** But there had been many skirmishes leading up to this, dating right back to the 12th century.

The two countries appear to be getting along together a lot better these days though.

We can't do a tour of France without mentioning **Joan of Arc, The Maid of Orléans -** 1412 - 1431.
This lady was the hero of the hour, during the hundred years war, but sadly burnt at the end,
She was born into poverty in **Domrémy-la-Pucelle** and died in **Rouen.**
She had a very confused and sad life.
Her main claim to fame appears to be that she was prone to having **'visions'.**

Superstition appears to have played a major part, both in her rise and in her downfall.

Joan went out of her way to attract attention and was held as a 'saviour' during a time of want where someone was needed to instil hope as the English armies were gaining ground.

Sadly her leadership abilities eventually fell apart.

Napoleon Bonaparte (15 August 1769 - 5 May 1821) will be one of the notable names that we think of in relation to France.

His attempt to world domination was going well until he overstepped his ambitions in a bid to overcome **Russia.**

Sadly for those who followed him, his ambitions were larger than his resources.

He ended his life in exile on the island of **Elba** just off the western coast of **Italy.**

The French Revolution:

Began in 1789 and lasted until 1794.

The main reason for the peasants' revolt was that of nationwide poverty and starvation.

To bring the crisis to a head King Louis XVI decided he needed more money.

The Guillotine was one of France's instruments of death during their years of **The Revolution.**

It was first used in 1792 in order to execute a highwayman named **Nicolas Jacques Pelletier.**

The stories of old ladies knitting garments of death whilst heads were separated from bodies originated in fictional stories written after this time but may have a grain of truth.

France is an enormous country.

One could spend a lifetime here and still not see the greatest part.

There are so many **Religious Sites, Roman Buildings** and **Ancient Monuments** here.
France is awash with **Historical Remnants** it is difficult to see the beauty amongst the relics.

Whilst these sites of interest must be indicated, spare some time to look aside to see and experience the wonderful landscapes and vistas that are **France.**

Places of interest:

Paris:
The **Capital City.**
Visitors to this town will understandably be attracted to:
The Louvre Museum and Art Gallery..
The Eiffel Tower.
The Arc De Triomphe.
The Notre Dame's Cathedral, sadly now mostly destroyed by fire during April 2019.
The Folies Bergère - 1869 is, amazingly, still in business.

There are also some amazing **Parks** and wonderful things to experience whilst walking along the **River Seine.**

Plenty of **Street Theatre** here during the summer months.

Hauts-de-France:

It is almost impossible to tour this northwestern area of France without being reminded of the first and second world wars in which many thousands lost their lives and many more had their lives irreversibly altered forever.

Indeed, here is a reminder of all of the wars that have ever been throughout history, and still continue today, as humanity attempts to pursue its own greed for more.

But there is also some wonderful countryside to discover and many sights and scenes that are little known.

Dunkirk:
On the **Belgian** border.
The third largest **Harbour** in **France.**
The Miracle of Dunkirk.
On 26th May until 4th June 1940 338,000 British and French soldiers were rescued from the beaches of **Dunkirk.**

Château de Chantilly:
A jewel of a castle.

Built by **Henri d'Orléans, Duke of Aumale**, the son of the last **King of France, who was Louis the XV1.** This castle is well worth spending a day at, it is quite marvellous.

Another time well spent would be at the amazing **La Cathédrale Saint-Pierre de Beauvais.**

The Coast of Normandy:

Stretching from **Le Tréport** in the north to **Mont St Michel** in the south.

Calvados:
The name comes not from the **French Spirit** that is manufactured here from **Apple Cider,** but from a group of sedimentary rocks on the shoreline.

Rouen:
The city of **'A Hundred Bell Towers'.**
The last resting place of **Joan of Arc.**
There is an amazing permanent **Market** here all year round.
An **Annual 'Belly' Food Festival** that you must not miss during the second and third weeks of October.
The houses in the streets are also extraordinary and well worth coming just for those alone.
There is such a vast variety and mixture dating from the early 1500's.
Rouen Cathedral is not to be sneezed at either.

Bayeux:

The **Bayeux Tapestry** is certainly worth the visit and will take approximately 1 and half hours to 2 hours to fully view it..

There are audio headsets in several languages.

There is a **Market** here on Wednesdays and Saturdays.

A Walk through **Old Bayeux** is always good to view the old buildings and architecture - Fascinating.

Notre-Dame de Bayeux Cathedral is interesting.

There is a **Battle of Normandy Museum** and a **Cemetery.**

Don't miss **The Weeping Beech** when you visit **The Botanical Gardens - 'The Tree of France'.**

Brittany:

Mont-St-Michel:

The site of a group of **Monastic Buildings** which were the centre for learning during the middle ages.

There is now a large community of people who live here permanently.

This is a tidal island so beware of getting back.

There is a twin to this magical island in **Cornwall** - **St. Michaels Mount**

Cancale:

On one of Brittany's craggy outposts is the very best place to collect, buy and to taste **Oysters!**

There are many **Fishy Restaurants** here.

This is also a great place for rock pools and exploring the beaches.

St. Malo:
A thriving seaside harbour and beach area.
This is a very picturesque walled city.
Very popular with tourists.

Carnac:
The south end of this coastal area is a long strip of sandy beach.
Most popular are **The Carnac Stones -** thousands of prehistoric standing stones spread across three alignments: **Ménec, Kermario** and **Kerlescan.**
I guess that all stones are prehistoric.
These particular stones just happened to be put in certain places by humans many years ago.

Reims:
Known in Roman times as - **Durocortorum.**
One of the most historic towns in **France.**
Vesle River runs alongside.
This is a great **Champagne** producing region so please don't go home thirsty.
Parc de Champagne - Destroyed during the first world war but rebuilt and redesigned.
Several old buildings here and some marvellous trees.
Reims-Champagne Automobile Museum:
This is one of the most visited museums in **Reims** and so exciting!!
Reims Cathedral:
Where around thirty Kings of France were crowned.

Reims Planetarium: - Only **£3.50** to enter and much more fun than the one in **London.**

The Palace of Tau:

Built in the 5th century to house bishops.

The Abbey of Saint-Remi.

An Abbey founded in the 11th century.

One of the great **Museums** of this area is **St. Remi History Museum.**

Visit the Villa Demoiselle:

A grand old house of France.

Wine tasting here and a superb opportunity to tour an original **Grande Chateaux.**

Hotel Le Vergeur Museum:

One of the oldest buildings in **Reims -** an opportunity to delve back into the 13th century.

Sainte Clotilde of Reims Basilica:

We all know what a **Basilica** is don't we?

Well, apparently, in catholic terms, it is a church that has been given certain special privileges.

But it certainly looks grand.

Mars Gate - Porte de Mars: - Some more superstition for you here.

Dating from the third century a.d. This was the widest arch in the Roman world.

How those Romans managed to put things together astounds me!

Verzenay Windmill:

19th century **Windmill** surviving on the windswept **Mont Rizan.**

Carnegie library.

This library takes its name because it was created by money donated from the Carnegie foundation.
Gallo-Roman Cryptoporticus:
Dating from the 3rd century. - A Roman passageway.

The Upper Rhine:

Strasbourg:
You must visit the Gothic **Cathédrale Notre-Dame de Strasbourg,** with its animated **Astronomical Clock** Sitting astride the **River Ill.**
Parc de l'Orangerie:
A great spot for a picnic to sit and view the **Storks Nesting** in early spring and also pay a visit to the **Zoo!**

Alsace:
Twelfth century **Château du Haut-Kœnigsbourg:**
An epic complex with views all the way to the **Black Forest.**
Only £8.00. Admission fee for a superb day in amongst some wonderful settings.

Troyes:
If you enjoy **Stained Glass Windows** this is the place for you.
There are a variety of **Museums** to enjoy here.
Wander through the narrow streets and enjoy the shopping treats.
Sample the famous **Andouillette of Troyes -** or if sausage isn't your choice - **Chaource Cheese.**

The Prunelle de Troyes (local liqueur), or **Pascal Caffet's Chocolate Confections**.

The Loire Valley:
Filled with vineyards and cycle trails.

The **Loire** is France's longest river.
Follow its meandering way from **Orléans** to **Angiers**.
There are more than **300 Grand Châteaux**.

Orléans:
It was here that **Joan of Arc** saved the city from an English siege in 1429.
There is an annual festival at the end of April to celebrate the fact.
Visit - **Maison de Jeanne-d'Arc -** A reconstructed house where the lady stayed during the siege.
A superb base for visiting **Vineyards** and **Castles**.
Le Parc Floral de la Source:
A great **Botanical Garden** by The **Loiret River**.
Free Croquet and **Badminton** and lots of different **Gardens**.
Don't miss the **Dahlia** and **Iris Gardens** or the **Vegetable Garden**.
Musée des Beaux-Arts:
Next door to the **Cathedral**.
There is a collection of paintings by artists like **Picasso, Van Dyck, Correggio, Velazquez, and Gauguin**.
Hotel Groslot:
A huge house built in 1550 -The home of **Francois II** who married **Mary, Queen of Scots**.

Only 30 minutes drive away is **The Orléans Forest.**
Spectacular walks.

Tours:
Magnificent mediaeval half timbered houses.
Saint-Gatien Cathedral and the **Renaissance Hôtel Goüin** are both notable but also enjoy the many restaurants and nightlife.

Angiers:
The mediaeval seat of the **Plantagenet Dynasty.**
It seems impossible to visit a single town or city in **France** without there being a **Cathedral** to tour.
The **Câtel d'Angiers** is a good day visit.
This is a proper castle to fall in love with.
Lotsof history and things to see and discover!
Terra Botanica is an experience you might not want to miss.
The adventure of plants.
A day out with a distinct difference. Lots of animations and adventures to get involved with - Great for children too!

La Rochelle:
Rocky and sandy beaches, some very private and peaceful.
Surfing, Surfing and surfing.
When you have had enough surfing, (as if that's a thing), there is a marvellous **Harbour** to **Fish** in or to take a boat out to sea.
The **Aquarium** will cost £15.00. But there's a lot to see.

Don't miss the **Maritime Museum** and **Parc Charruyer** with a little river.

Les Halles de La Rochelle - Every morning this market is filled with goodies.

On Wednesdays and Saturdays it overflows into the main square.

Bordeaux:

We all know **Bordeaux** for being the wine-growing region that it certainly is.

It is alo a very busy **Port City** set on the **River Garonne.**

The Grand Place de la Bourse surrounds the **Three Graces Fountain.**

Do not miss the **Miroir d'Eau -** reflecting pool.

There is a very **Gothic Cathédrale Saint-André.**

Art Museums , one of which is the **Musée des Beaux-Arts de Bordeaux.**

There are **Public Gardens** along the **River.**

During the first week of August you will not want to miss the **Bordeaux Open Air Jazz Festival.**

There is a very grand **Opera House** for your entertainment.

A **Sea Marine Museum.**

The Port Cailhau, thirty-five metres tall, is integrated into the city walls.

Dating from 1864 - a great place for views of **Bordeaux.**

Dordogne:

This area has some of the most beautiful villages in all of France.

Collonges-la-Rouge has got to be one of the prettiest among those.

There are also **Gorges, Rocky Plateau and Caves.**

Gouffre de Padirac is the most amazing **Cave System.**

After dropping from 75 feet we are able to board a boat for the rest of the journey.

On top of many amazing features, during the journey you will come upon **The Salle du Grand Dôme** with its 94 metre high ceiling.

The Tours de Merle will be one of the highlights here.

A fantastic day out.

Look out for **Jousting** and **Jugglers, Court Jesters** and **Mediaeval Mock Battles.**

Check out the events when booking online.

Château des Anglais in Autoire - An English Castle in not too bad nick!

Built during the **Hundred Years War.**

Lyon:

The gourmet capital of France.

In the city centre you will discover **Place Bellecour.**

There are over 2000 years of history here.

Begin the visit with **The Roman Amphithéâtre des Trois Gaules.**

There is also **Mediaeval** and **Renaissance Architecture** in **Vieux (Old Lyon).**

You will enjoy **The 'Traboules' -** Covered passageways between buildings which connect **Vieux Lyon** and **La Croix-Rousse Hill.**

The Parc de la Tête d'or, or **The Park of the Golden Head.**

This is a lovely little park and for an added bonus there is also a **Free Zoo!**

With giraffes, deer, reptiles, primates, along with other animals and a **Mini Train - Toot Toot!**

Haute-Savoie Région:

Tucked up beneath **The Alps**.

Ideal for year round **Ski Lifts** and access to the **Aiguilles de Chamonix Mountain Range** and the mighty **Mont Blanc.**

Thonon-les-Bains:

A multicultural **Harbour Town** on the banks of **Lake Geneva.**

There are delightful hilltop walks amongst the greenery. **Saint-Hippolyte Church Is** interesting as is **Saint-François-de-Sales Basilica.**

Avoriaz:

In truth this area is naturally ideal for winter sports and all that is white.

This is one of those most popular centres.

But if you do turn up in the spring and summer months, take the opportunity to hike.

In doing so you have a great chance to discover the **Marmots** who dwell on the mountainsides.

For a lot of fun and laughter visit nearby Lindarets to experience the goats village where goats roam free during the summer months.

Enjoy the hair raising drive to our next stop…..

Aiguille du Midi:
This is the highest you can get without hiking or climbing.
The highest of aerial lifts.
An excellent view of the peaks of **Mont Blanc.**

Annecy:
A town of canals and wonderful walks.
You will be thrilled by it's **'Old Town'** with cobbled streets and arches
Châteaux-de-Annecy - A restored **Castle** which has been transformed into a **Museum.**
Lake Annecy - The most picturesque and photographed lake in all of Europe.
Here you can enjoy guided walks.
Long evening strolls, biking, boating, waterskiing, sailboarding, you name it.
Visit some of the quaint **Old World Villages** spread around its shores or simply relax on the **Beaches.**

Provence:
Bounded by **Lower Rhone** to the west, **The Durance** to the north, **The Alps** to the east and including the **French Riviera** to the south.

An absolutely superb area of France renowned for its vineyards and countryside.
Wonderfully friendly inhabitants and very pretty villages.
Almost untouched for hundreds of years.

'A year in Provence' is a book that will set the scene very nicely for this area.

The Lower Rhone Valley:

Orange:
Don't miss **The Roman Amphitheatre** and **The Triumphal Arch of Orange.**

Carpentras:
The best market in France!!
Since 1155, this town has hosted one of the largest markets in **Provence.**
Over 350 stands take over the streets of the old town every Friday morning

Avignon:
Shall we sing this one together?
On the bridge at **Avignon**…

Sur le Pont d'Avignon
L'on y danse, l'on y danse
Sur le Pont d'Avignon
L'on y danse tous en rond.

Les beaux messieurs font comme ça
Et puis encore comme ça.

Les belles dames font comme ça
Et puis encore comme ça.

One of the most notable sites to visit at **Avignon** is **The Palais des Papes.**

It is a residence, a monastery, the seat of power and a fortress all in one.

The size of five castles or cathedrals, a sight well worth a day's outing with no less than 25 rooms open to the public.

Nîmes:

Les Jardins de la Fontaine may well be your first stop here.

An excellent choice too. A wonderful garden setting alongside the river with plenty of **Follies** and **Roman Statues** to break up the walk.

You will not go short of **Roman Architecture** here but do not miss the wonderful **Pont du Gard.**

The highest standing **Roman Aqueduct** in the world, Next, catch up with the roman history of **Nimes** by watching a film inside **La Maison Carrée**, literally **'The Square House'.**

It is one of the best-preserved **Roman Temples** in the world. Built around 16 BC,

The Arena can not be missed as it is one of the best preserved **Amphitheatres** there is to be seen.

There are also several very well laid out **Museums** in **Nimes** as well as **Great Restaurants**, **Bars** and **Walks.**

Arles:

A taste of **Rome** without the crowds.

Arles is an excellent all rounder.

There is so much **Roman Architecture** to see here and yet a wonderfully laid back atmosphere.

The **Roman Amphitheatre** here could seat 21,000 people!!

Vincent Van Gogh has strong links here too.

Some of his most famous paintings such as **'the 'Sunflowers', 'The Yellow House'** and his **'Bedroom in Arles'** were all completed here.

Visit the **Cryptoporticus** in the bowels of the city, deep underground.

The French Riviera: The Côte d'Azur:

If you are spending much time around this area to visit sites, get the **'Côte d'Azur France Pass'**.

Many Euros can be saved by doing so.

There is also a separate **Marseilles 'City Pass'**.

Marseilles:

Marseilles is a sea port with a difference.

This is at the top end of glamorous sea ports.

The oldest city in France.

It was established by Greek settlers from Phocaea in 600 BC.

If it is a beach you are looking for, try**:**

Prophet's Beach.

Prado Beach.

Catalan Beach.

The most interesting and attractive sites of **Marseilles** can all be reached on foot from a starting point at the

Mucem, the Museum of European and Mediterranean Civilisations.

The Old Port is within reach from here too, where the most popular tourist areas are.

The Chateau d'If is a worthwhile visit - take a boat trip from the harbour. It is an excellent **Fortress** built on an island. It featured in the famous book by **Alexander Dumas - The Count of Monte Cristo.**

Enjoy the **Old Prison** here too.

The Fort Saint Jean is one of the most important and popular sites to see and, amazingly, **it is free!**

There are also plenty of **Churches** and a **Cathedral** as well as **Fine Art Galleries** and **Museums** aplenty.

Saint-Tropez:

Another very glamorous fishing port.

It was an abode of artists and the very famous during the sixties.

Its beaches and nightlife are the reason for its continued popularity.

If you are looking for very valuable yachts then the old fishing port is the place to be.

Cannes:

Famous for the annual **International Film Festival.**

The beaches are soft, golden and sandy, you will need to rise very early to find a space.

There are plenty of well stocked boutiques and hotels.

Grasse:

Known worldwide as the centre of **Perfume.**

This is the birthplace.

If you are at all interested in the **Perfume Industry** you will want to visit here.

Here you can make your own **Perfume** and enter a course to develop your **'Nose'.**

There are over 2000 different perfumes that can all be selectively distinguished from each other.

Visit the perfume houses of **Fragonard, Molinard,** and **Galimard.**

Get lost in the **'Old Town'** the streets and alleys are fascinating.

Nice:

An elegant town.

The Musée Matisse is a very fine **Art Gallery.**

The Promenade des Anglais is known to a world wide audience.

This is the place to see all that is happening on the beaches below.

It runs for seven kilometres and is a good walk to be had after a heavy meal.

Henri Matisse was once a resident here.

Èze:

The enchanting village of **Eze**, looking more **Italian** than **French.**

This spectacular village is perched on a hilltop overlooking the **Mediterranean Sea.**

The drive along the coast to get here is worth the visit.

There is much serenity and beauty here, particularly if you arrive early.

There are no cars allowed in the centre.

En route to **Spain** - On the **A75 Autoroute** If travelling directly from the north:
Millau:
The Millau Viaduct - A must drive over and stop.
Many tourists heading to southern France and Spain follow this route because it is direct and without tolls for the 340 kilometres (210 mi) between **Clermont-Ferrand** and **Béziers**.

There is parking and an information and viewing area on the north side.
It was designed by a British architect; it is the largest viaduct in the world.
Taller in places than the **Eiffel Tower**.

Perpignan:
Known as the '**Catalan Capital**'.
Not quite **French** or **Spanish** but very **Catalan**.
Catalan is widely spoken here. The same language that is spoken in **Barcelona**.
Once the capital of **The Kingdom of Majorca**.
Visit **The Palace of The Kings of Majorca**.
Do not miss **The Castillet**. It is a part of the city's walls and was once **A Prison**.
Musée Hyacinthe-Rigaud will fill your appetite for both historical data and art.
Marché Cassanyes is the market to go to in **Perpignan**.

It takes place every day at **Place des Cassanyes** from 07:30 to 13:30.
It is packed with every conceivable Mediterranean goodie.

The walled city of **Carcassonne:**
An excellent town to visit.
The **Walled Fortifications** and **Watchtowers** are astounding! - Initially built 100 years before Jesus was born.
Built on a hill.
Visit **Carcassonne Castle** too.
Carcassonne is famous for its **Duck Foie Gras, Foies Secs -** a traditional pork liver recipe, and **Languedoc-style Snails** also **Corbières Wild Boar Stew**
There are some excellent daily markets here too.

Toulouse:
You may wish to drop south from here to experience the mighty **Pyrenees Mountains** and to pop into the tax haven and duty free country of **Andorra** for some shopping.

Toulouse is known as **'The Pink City'** as a consequence of the pink hue derived from the 'terra cotta' bricks used in many of its buildings.
It sits on the **Mighty Garonne River.** On which you could enjoy a **Cruise.**
The Museum de Toulouse would be a good place to begin exploring.

Jardin Japonais is due north of the centre and a very peaceful place to wander around.

La Basilique Saint-Sernin is interesting. It sits on an Abbey that was in use during the 800's. There are relics that were donated by **Charlemane**. As is the **Place du Capitole** with its frescoes and architecture.

The Cité de l'Espace is a theme park that concentrates on space adventure.

Feeling hungry?

Cassoulet is a delicious casserole that is one of the specialities around this region.

The Basque Country:

There are seven distinct areas within the **Basque Country,** four of these are in **Northern Spain**, where ninety percent of Basque speakers live and three in **South Western France.**

The three **Basque** areas in **France** are very loosely, (and fiercely disputed), **Labourd,** with the historical capital of **Ustaritz.**

Lower Navarre with its historical capitals of **Saint-Jean-Pied-de-Port** and **Saint-Palais** with its historical capital **Mauléon.**

Euskara, which is the **Basque Language,** is linguistically distinct from French, Spanish or any other language.

Bayonne:

The largest festival in all of **France - The Annual Bayonne Festival** has been enjoyed since 1932.
It is held at the end of July each year and lasts for four days.
The **Nive River** is at the centre of this city and it is lined with many restaurants, bars and shops.
Although technically a city there is no hustle and bustle.
A leisurely walk or sit in **Jardin Botanique,** can be enjoyed in relative peace.
The Musée Basque is one of the first ports of call here, displaying a wide example of the arts and crafts that are native to this area as well as a good history.
By the **Nive River** you will find the covered market of Bayonne - **"Les Halles"**.
You will find meat, fish and a couple of bakeries, where you can try the tasty **Gâteau Basque.**
Jews escaping from the Spanish inquisition during the 17 century introduced **Chocolate Making** to this area and contributed to its growth and wealth.

Biarritz:
Made popular when surfing was 'invented' here during the 1950's.
A **Surfers** paradise with sandy beaches and plenty of surf.
Good views over the **Bay of Biscay** from the cliff tops too.
The City Ocean Museum and **The Aquarium** are both excellent.
The Grande Plage is known as 'the playground of the rich and famous'.

St Jean-de-Luz:
On the Spanish Border.
Sunny, sandy golden beaches.
Made famous for its association with **Pirates (Corsairs)** during the 17th century.
Once one of the busiest ports in France.

Our zig zag route through **France** has included a fair part of the country.
We hope you've enjoyed the journey and strayed a little too!
Our route has left us at the doorstep of their southern neighbour - **Spain.**

Monaco:

A sovereign city-state and microstate on the **French Riviera.**

Neither in Schengen or the E.U. but cannot be entered without travelling through France and so follows, and is governed largely by, those rules.

Places of interest:

There is the coastal view of millionaires' yachts.

Being a very tiny, expensive and wealthy state most places of interest relate to eating and luxurious living.

Monaco is known mainly for the **Grand Prix Racing** held here each spring and **Rallying** during January.

There is a regular **Yacht Show** during September.

The **Casino de Monte-Carlo** Is well known and made famous by **David Niven** in the comedy film **Casino Royale** and **Ian Fleming** as the inventor of **James Bond,** a fictional spy in a book of the same name written in 1953.

The Prince's Palace is a site that can be visited and toured for a fee of just under £9.00.

Corsica:

One of the 18 regions of France.
The fourth largest Island in the Mediterranean.

Very close to **Sardinia.**

There are regular and frequent ferries that run between these two islands; the journey can take as little as 50 minutes.

The climate tends to be warm during most of the year with rainy spells in the winter.

It has an **Italian** culture but has been a part of **France** since 1768.

The native **Corsican Language** is **Corsu** but **French** and **Italian** are generally spoken in tourist areas.

The inland areas are mostly craggy and mountainous - The highest peak is **Monte Cinto** at 2,706 metres (8,878 feet) high.

Places of Interest:

There are sandy beaches available on all sides of the coast.
Some are very popular like the **Pietracorbara** and some less so like **Saleccia** and **Rondinara.**
Loto, in the north, is a good beach for **Snorkelling.**

The Grande Randonnée No. 20 - Better known as the **GR20**, is an **112 Mile Long Hiking Trail** over the roughest terrain through the **Corsica Regional Nature Reserve.**
It is renowned for being the **Toughest Hiking Trail** in Europe.

The Corsica Regional Nature Park:
Extends over 350,510 hectares - about 40% of the island.
Amongst which you can discover **The Col de Bavella Pass,** many **Mountain Lakes, The Nature Reserve of Scandola** and **The Restonica Gorges.**

There are **Three Train Routes** that tour the island. Any one of which will reveal some spectacular views and a good comfortable way to get around too.

There are many opportunities to view the **Rugged Coastline** and also the impressive **Ancient Buildings** from the sea by booking a boat ride from any of the fishing ports on the island.

Ajaccio:
The birthplace of **Napoleon Bonaparte.**

Bonifacio:
An excellent **Citadel** overlooking the **Walled Town.**

Calvi:

Has a wonderful **Marina** and loads of sandy beaches.

Andora:

The rules regarding both Schengen and visas are quite vague in Andorra.
No visas are required for tourists on visits less than 90 days.
Checks at the borders or within their borders, regarding time spent there, are very rare.

Andorra is unique and bizarre in very many ways which suits its geographical position.

For more detailed information go here:

https://andorraguides.com/visa/schengen/#:~:text=facto%20to%20Andorra.-,Tourist%20Visa%20for%20Andorra,must%20be%20carried%20for%20entry.

Or here:
andorraguides.com

Famous for Ski slopes, gigantic natural parks, and top-notch duty-free shopping.

My children love driving up to **Andorra** from **Barcelona** simply for the ride.
The mountain scenery is terrific!

Places of interest:

Grandvalira - Ski resort

Casa de la vall - **Museum**

Mirador Roc Del Quer Canillo:
Superb views
Parc Central:
Very peaceful park and gardens - worth a visit

Ski Station Pal-Arinsal, Vallnord - Skiing

Pont de Paris:
Iconic bridge - great view point and of **Salvador's Dali's Melting Clock.**

National Automobile Museum:
Pretty much does what it says on the tin.
Unless you are a keen enthusiast don't allow more than an hour to take this in.

There is much scenic beauty in **Andorra** everywhere.
Take time to explore - set off on a trek.

Portugal:

Schengen rules apply.
90 day maximum stay in E.U. applies.

On the **Iberian Peninsula.**

Very friendly towards U.K. citizens having historically shared **Spain** as a common enemy.

Fish dishes are a specialty throughout the country.

Places of interest:

Porto:
The Dom Luis I Bridge.
Rua Santa Caterina Church.
Douro River.
Drive or even cruise through the **Douro Valley**.

Lisbon:
The **Capital City** and hub of activity.
To arrive on the other side of the **Tagus Estuary**, drive over **The Ponte Vasco da Gama -** It is truly a breathtaking event.
It is the second longest bridge in Europe, after the **Crimean Bridge,**
You must also admire and drive over the **Ponte 25 de Abril Suspension Bridge** for the same reasons.

Vasco da Gama (1460-1524) sailed from here in 1497 on a mission to reach **India** and open a sea route from Europe to the East.
Museums here are filled with amazing information on Portugal and its fascinating history.
See the **National Azulejo Museum.**
The Jerónimos Gothic Monastery is interesting.
Visit **Castelo São Jorge.**
The best tour in **Lisbon** and well worth the money - including **Ramparts** and **Watchtowers** and **Gardens** too.
The entrance fee isn't included in the **Lisbon Card,** which is a shame, but still good value.
There are spectacular views from the **Ramparts.**
Lisbon has several wonderful **Markets:**
Here are a few well worth experiencing:
Mercado da Ribeira. (Fresh Market). Whilsthere sample some of the wares at **Manteigaria**, which makes some of the best **Pastéis** anywhere.
Time Out Market - The largest food hall in Lisbon.
Mercado 31 de Janeiro - The place for **Seafood -** an excellent **Fish Restaurant** here too!
You must ride through Lisbon's streets, on a tram, at least once!
Visit the **Baxai District,** the **Alfama District** and **The Belem District** too if you have time.

Evora:
Evora Roman Temple.
Local cuisine - **Porco Preto -** 'Black Pork'.

Sines:
The birthplace of **Vasco da Gama.**
The beaches here are quiet and spacious.
You will love **A Reserva Natural das Lagoas de Santo André e da Sancha.**
Just 20 minutes north of **Sines.**

Faro:
Lots of islands to visit from here.
Wander around **Ria Formosa Island.**
And **Barreta Island** - Excellent for bird watching.
Faro's quaint **Old Town.**

We have concentrated mainly on the west coastal areas but there is also a wealth of places to visit if you wish to travel inland to savour the less frequented areas, quaint villages, friendly locals, always willing to stop for a chat or give local advice.

Spain:
España:

Schengen rules apply.
90 day maximum stay in E.U. applies.

Best to visit during the cooler spring and winter months to avoid the crowds.
.
The sites and sounds of **Spain** are far too varied and wonderful to list them all within these few pages.

A whole book would not be sufficient to cover all there is to see in this vast area.

The country has been welded together from a complex mix of cultures and communities.
Visit the land of the **Catalans** who still strive for independence.

Catalonia is to be discovered in the north east of **Spain**.
Roughly an area bordering, and including south eastern **France** and **Andorra** down to **Amposta** in the south.

There are four languages spoken in this area:
Catalan.
Spanish.
Aranese - A dialect of Occitan spoken in the **Aran Valley** - An area north of **'Lleida'** (Catalan) or **'Lérida'**.
Catalan Sign Language.

The **Basques** in the north have their own language, unlike any other, and live in a country within a country.

Watch the **'Human Towers'** being erected at various **Festivities** and **Carnivals.**

From **Barcelona** to **Seville.** From **Bilbao** to **Madrid** and on to **Murcia.**

There are mountains of snow and deserts of sand.
Warm seas and bustling markets.

The peoples, customs, dialects and languages of Spain also are varied from the north to the south and east to west.
Explore and enjoy this wonderful country.

Places of interest:

Our route will take the shape of an inverted **'S'** to remind us of where we are **(Spain).**
I guess we could have planned an **'E'** but with fuel costs being as they are we worked with an **'S'.**

We will begin with **Spain's Capital City** and then return to the north to work our way down towards **The Straits of Gibraltar,** from north to south - zigzagging along the way.

Madrid:
Spain's Capital City.

Let us start with **Puerta del Sol:**
The main square and the very place to begin a tour.
Most sites are within walking distance of this fabulous,
semi circular square such as **Plaza Mayor, Arenal,
Alcalá** and **Preciados.**

It is also the place where most major road routes in
Spain begin.

Retiro Park:
A wonderful **Free** place to come in order to breathe
fresh air and to chill out..

The Great Pond is wonderful for boat rides, it has been
host to royalty doing exactly that.

Here on weekends you will be joined by **Musicians,
Street Artists** and **Stalls** of all kinds.

The Crystal Palace was inspired by the same glass
building in London.

There are many other **Follies, Statues** and **Fountains**
in this voluptuous Park.

There are several very different **Gardens** and **Avenues**
here.

Royal Palace:
The official residence of the royal family.
It has stood on this site for three hundred years.
Entrance is free to members of the European Union and
some other visitors, check before you go.

Museo del Prado - Regarded as the finest **Art Gallery**
in the world.

Plaza Mayor:
You can enter this area by walking through one of **Ten
Archways** and then look up at the **237 Balconies**
overlooking the plaza.

It is home to the annual **Christmas Market**.
It has also hosted bullfights and soccer games.
On a Sunday visit **El Rastro Market**.
At the **Plaza Cascorro**.
There will be more than 1,000 street vendors and a very busy time.
Come early to bag a bargain.

Santiago de Compostela:
In the north west, is the capital of Spain's **Galicia Region.**
It's known as the culmination of the **Camino de Santiago Pilgrimage Route** and the 'alleged' burial site of St. James - **The Cathedral** will be the place to view this and other tombs.
Alameda Park is an exciting place to be out in the open and a breath of loveliness.
This is a park not to be sneezed at.
Full of a variety of species and areas.
I have found few that can be compared with its vastness.
There is a surprise to be found around every corner.
You could spend a few days discovering this gem.
The Monastery of San Martiño Pinario:
This is a **Benedictine Monastery -** The second largest in Spain.

Picos de Europa National Park:
Reaching out over the areas of **Asturias, Cantabria and León** and including 11 villages.

Home to many **Birds of Prey,** including, **Griffon Vultures, Golden, Short-toed and Booted Eagles, Egyptian Vultures, Kites, Kestrels and Peregrine Falcons.**

There are also some very wild animals that live here such as the **Iberian Wolf**.

There are over 2,500 of them here and the **Brown Bear.**

You will need to look carefully if you want to see the elusive **Pyrenean Desman** and there are also over 70 other mammals that wander through this forested and mountainous area.

The highest peak here is the **Torre de Cerredo** at a height of 2,650 metres.

There is a **Cable Car** to the very top for those of us who prefer a little less exercise, from **Fuente Dé,** about 20 km west of **Potes.**

There are plenty of treks around the park but we think the most beautiful and worthwhile, if we had to pick only one, is **Cares Gorge Hike,** or **The Ruta del Cares.**

It follows the **Cares River** and has lots of amazing little bridges to cross.

It is around 7.5 km and can easily be completed in a day.

There are also some gorgeously, pretty villages, including **Posada de Valdeón** which has a **National Park Office.**

Cantabria:

The Ebre Delta:

There are few words that can easily describe the magnificence of **The Ebro Valley** and **The Ebro Delta.** A slow tour, from its springs at **Fontibre** near **Reinosa** in the **Cantabrian Mountains,** along this river to **Amposta** in **Southern Catalonia**, is a must.

Hiking the whole route would be my advice but if you are driving, please take the minor roads in order to explore **The Ebro** fully.

By way of explanation:
'Ebro' is the Spanish and **Basque pronunciation, The Catalan is 'Ebre'**

Fontibre:
To visit the **Karst Springs** that are the beginnings of the mighty **Ebro River** call in at the visitor centre - **Centro de Visitantes del Río Ebro**, which gives much information on its history.
This is a very picturesque area.

Logroño:
If you are a wine lover or oenophile, you will love this area, the vineyards stretch as far as you can see.
It is on the pilgrims route to **Santiago de Compostela.** But more interestingly for us, it is situated on the **Ebro River.**
The Paseo del Príncipe de Vergara is to be found just outside the old town and is an oasis of quiet peacefulness and shade.

La Rioja Museum will take you on a journey from prehistoric times through to the 20th century.

Sta. Mª de La Redonda Pro Cathedral.

The twin towers, built by Martín de Berriatúa, are worth seeing.

Puente de Piedra Bridge - One of four bridges over the **Ebre.**

Los Peregrinos Fountain.

Near Nuévalos:

The Monasterio de Piedra (the **Park and Falls**, not the hotel).

This is another of those absolutely **'must do visits'.**

Indescribable **Natural Waterfalls** of every description along a wooded valley of such great depth.

You will need strong boots and plenty of water to keep you hydrated.

Zaragoza:

A beautiful 200 year old town on the **River Ebro** with lots to offer, including several museums and many Roman archaeological remains.

To see:

The Old Roman Forum.

The Teatro Romano.

The Ancient City Walls.

There is a super **Cathedral,** I wouldn't believe all, or anything that is said about the Apostle James in connection with it though.

Whether James actually ever visited Spain or not is debatable, but from his teachings and the teachings of Jesus, we can be sure that ornate and expensive buildings were not, even remotely, to be desired.

Jesus taught that His kingdom is built with people who have been born again and are living in good relationships with each other and not buildings of any size.

The Central Market is a two story building and a great place to find fresh fruit and vegetables, freshly baked goods and deli products.

Huesca:
Mostly a wild and mountainous area.
Very few people live anywhere outside of **Huesca**, therefore it has not been spoiled by 'progress' as many places have.
Aragonese is widely spoken here.
It is the birthplace of the **Ancient Kingdom of Aragon**, the most powerful empire of the Mediterranean during the Middle Ages.
Here you will find **The Palace of Aragonese Kings.**

Only one hour north of here, on the French border, you must visit **The National Park of Ordesa** and **Monte Perdido.**
The tallest mountain in the Pyrenees and highest limestone massif in Europe. - **The Aneto** is here which has many **Glaciers**, such as at **Monte Perdido.**

You can be lost in the wonders of these valleys for a lifetime.

Catalonia:

Lleida (Catalan) or **Lérida** (Spanish):
Catalan is the spoken language here and throughout **Catalonia.**
Established on **The Segre River.**
La Seu Vella - A Gothic-Romanesque Cathedral is interestingly situated in a ruined hilltop fortress - **Castle of the King (La Suda) -** Refuge of the last **Caliph of Cordoba.**
On a hill to the west is the 12th-century **Castle of Gardeny Complex -** A military fortress dating back to the **Knights Templar** exploits in this region.

Barcelona:
The best way to see Barcelona is on foot.
It is a fairly large city but easily explored during one or two days.
The town is understandably captivated by the artist **Antoni Gaudi** who lived and died here.
The expiatory temple of the **Sagrada Familia** that he commenced building in 1882 is estimated to be completed in approximately one hundred years time.
Millions of tourists queue to tour this site each year.
The Gaudi Park - Park Güell, composed of gardens and architectural elements located on Carmel Hill is to be complimented and recommended.
La Pedrera Is another not to be missed.

Casa Batlló is one of the absolute best museum shops you could enter.

Las Ramblas - Begin at the bottom, walk to the top and then walk back down to the bottom again.
As you go up the hill, on the left, look out for the lady in red waving her handkerchief at you from her balcony.
But do not be distracted by her charm.
There are plenty of street theatre actors and other amazing things going on as you walk and stop and walk some more.
La Boqueria Market - off **Las Ramblas** is a 'must not be missed' visit.
A massive undercover market filled with the biggest, freshest, most sumptuous fruit and veg that was ever seen. Plus a meat market and various other stalls as well.
One could easily spend a day simply experiencing this.
There are plenty of cafes and coffee bars to spend time in here too.
You will not be able to avoid seeing plenty of **Gaudi's** work around the town.
It is everywhere, there are 14 buildings built by him in Barcelona alone.
And there are plenty of opportunities to explore the museums exhibiting his artwork.
Ciutadella Park is somewhat amazing.
Filled with fantastic waterfalls and fountains of every type, shape, colour and design.
There are also many follies and rivers and lakes.

Parc de Montjüic has the best views from its peak. Take the cable car to the top.
When you have seen enough of **Antoni Gaudi's** work visit the **Picasso Museum.**

Costa Daurada:

Now take the coastal road to:

Tarragona:
A wonderful Harbour town
The Amfiteatre de Tarragona is a fine **Roman Theatre** that would have housed 15,000 people.
The Rambla Nova in the main town is a good way to begin a tour of the shops. It is a 45 metre wide avenue, lined with palm trees and benches.
Visit **The National Archaeological Museum of Tarragona.**

Reserva Natural de Sebes:
More than 200 different species of birds have been observed in **Reserva Natural de Sebes.**
White Stork, Common Kingfisher, Purple Heron, Grey Heron, Water Rail, Lesser Spotted Woodpecker are some of the birds that nest in the reserve.
Among the birds of prey that nest - Black Kite and Marsh Harrier.

Caspe:
We have taken a detour here to arrive back at the **Ebro River**.

Are you enjoying your trek?

The **Ebro** is one of the most popular, cleanest and best places to fish in this area.

The largest fish ever caught and recorded here was a **Mirror Carp of 83lb**

This is a great place to park or even stay for the night, on one of the many campsites on the riverside.

The food here is excellent too.

Amposta:

Touring here you can't fail to see the miles of olive groves and fruit trees and farm produce being transported.

We have arrived at the **Ebro Delta.**

One of the most fertile areas in Spain.

A veritable breadbasket.

If you venture to the coast here you will be sure to see miles of **Flamingos** on the sandy shores.

There are in fact 95 different species of bird that breed here and 343 types of bird have been spotted.

Take time to see the **Suspension Bridge** at **Amposta**.

It wasn't built until 1915 and went a long way to join this area with **Valencia** and **Barcelona.**

Valencia:

Don't forget to get the **Valencia Card** here for discounts and free entry to the many **Museums, Art Galleries** and other sites.

Park on the harbour, it's free, and partake of a delicious **Paella** - They always taste better by the sea.

This area is famous for them.

It is a must to visit **- Ciudad de las Artes y las Ciencias - The City of Arts and Sciences** is a cultural and architectural complex and one of the 12 treasures of Spain.

Mercado Central de Valencia.

Located in the centre of town it is the largest fresh produce market in Europe.

L'Oceanogràfic is an **Oceanarium** by **The Turia River** on the southeast of the city.

Castilla–La Mancha:

The scene of the book **"Don Quixote"** by **Miguel de Cervantes.**

The area encompasses **Plains** dotted with **Vineyards, Castles** and **Windmills,** plus **Mountain Ranges.**

Cuenca:

A city set in the mountains and originally founded by the **Moors.**

Below are the deep gorges of the rivers **Huécar** and **Júcar.**

It is a walled town which is well worth exploring.

The town is famous for its **'Hanging Houses' - The Casas Colgadas -** Cantilevered over **The Huécar**

Gorge, they look like they are clinging to the cliffs' edges.

There is an interesting **Cathedral** here and **The Ciudad Encantada** - wind driven rock formations, which are even more fascinating.

Food - Ask for **Morteruelo,** an unusual stew that is very thick and mushed up and is usually made using 3 birds (partridge, quail and chicken) and 3 meats (hare, rabbit and pork), thickened with breadcrumbs and spiced with thyme and rosemary.

Toledo:

Another very ancient Moorish walled town.

Look out for the mediaeval Arab, Jewish and Christian monuments on the walls around the town.

Watching over **Toledo** is the **Alcázar de Toledo,** a former fortress housing a **Military Museum**

The **Bisagra Gate** and the **Sol Gate** open into the old quarter, where the **Plaza de Zocodover** is a lively meeting place.

Madrid:

See above.

Segovia:

Alcazar Castle was the inspiration for Walt Disney's **Cinderella's Castle** and it doesn't take much imagination to see why.

The Roman Aqueduct here must be one of the best. Enjoy a view from the top of this one, the steps up are by the **Tourist Office**

Take a walk along the walls of the town.

The Jewish Quarter in the south, still occupied by a mainly Jewish community, is one of the top places to spend some time window shopping and enjoying the culture and architecture.

Juan Bravo Theatre.

Juan Bravo (1483–1521) was a leader of a 16th-century **Castillion** revolt in Spain.

Mirador de la Pradera de San Marcos Park

Great place to come for views of the Castle.

Segovia Museum:

There are at least nine museums here but by far the best, depending upon your preferences, is **The Segovia,** previously known as the regional museum, which is also responsible for the **Zuloaga Museum.**

The Calle Juan Bravo gives a superb view of the heart of **Segovia** town

The Cathedral costs £ 3.44 to enter.

Salamanca:

The Battle of Salamanca (in French and Spanish known as **The Battle of the Arapile**s) on 22 July 1812 was a battle in which an Anglo-Portuguese army under the **Earl of Wellington** defeated **Marshal Auguste Marmont's** French forces at **Arapile,** during the Peninsular War.

A Spanish division was also present but took no part in the battle.

It is known as **The Golden City** because of the sandstone that is used in the construction of buildings here.

Salamanca Cathedral is rated as being one of the best. There is quite a youthful feeling to this town, partly due to its being the the site of one of Spain's oldest **Universities,** founded in the 1100's.

The Roman Bridge of Salamanca over the **River Tormes** is a good reminder of its past.

The Casa de las Conchas is a restored 1483 house with 400 scalloped shells on its walls.

Merida:

A marvellous town.

You will find a **Merida Card** indispensable here with so many sites to visit.

Founded by The Romans just 25 years before Jesus.

It encompasses more notable Roman sites than any other city.

These include the fabulous, still used, **Teatro Romano,** which has a double tier of columns rising onstage.

The Anfiteatro (amphitheatre) is connected to this.

The Circo Romano - Where gladiator fights and chariot races were held.

The Ancient Puente Romano - a 792m bridge spanning **The Río Guadiana.**

The Alcazaba - Which is a 9th-century **Islamic Fortress** built over Roman walls.

The National Museum of Roman Art is a must visit.

All of which tells you little about the town and people who live here - a treat you will have to discover yourself.

Andalusia:

Seville:

Sits on **The River Guadalquivir.**

Is a good base for touring **Andalusia:**

Spend some time in **The Plaza de España** situated within **The Parque de María Luisa.**

The riverside views and the surrounding architecture and people wandering past are all amazing.

An added bonus is that all this is free in this very expensive city.

The Royal Alcázars of Seville was built for **King Peter of Castile** on the site of a muslim fortress. One might get the impression that its builders were trying to get a message across.

You must take the opportunity to experience some **Flamenco Dancing** here.

Wander around the area of **Barrio Santa Cruz** to explore some famous sites there.

Visit the **Cathedral,** one of the worlds largest.

The Murallas de Sevilla - The Walls of Seville are quite remarkable and have seen a few skirmishes since they were built.

Huelva:

On the **Costa de la Luz**, sitting next to its neighbour, **Portugal.**

Huelva is the **Port** that in 1492 **Christopher Columbus** set sail from to discover America and new and prosperous lands.

There are lots of **Museums** here and some wonderful **Seafood Restaurants.**

As well as great beaches and shopping centres.

Cadiz:

The oldest city in western Europe.
Established around 1,100 years before Jesus.
A Harbour town with a coast filled with sandy beaches.
It is often believed that **Christopher Columbus,** the explorer, was **Spanish** but he was born in **Italy.**
However, as well as **Portugal,** he lived much of his life in **Spain** here in **Cadiz,** where he opened a book shop selling maps and charts.
Castillo de Santa Catalina - A 17th century castle which has served its time as a prison.
The Cadiz Street Carnival - 11 days of 'fun' and excitement, during the middle of February is one of the world's most famous, second only to **Rio.**

Córdoba:

In May you can enjoy **The Feria de los Patios.**
The only place in Spain that celebrates this flower festival.
Whilst travelling look out for the miles and miles of **Olive Plantations.**
Córdoba is world renowned for its **Leather Manufacturing** sites and **Silversmiths.**
Also the place of birth of the grand Roman philosopher **Seneca.**

Ronda:
A spectacular mountain top city.
Puente Nuevo - The longest bridge in Spain.
A magnificent structure completed in 1793.
I would travel the length of Spain just for this one site.
The newest and largest of three bridges that span the 120-metre-deep chasm that carries the **Guadalevín River**
The Mondragón Palace is one of the most impressive and historic buildings in the town.
It was built in the 14th century by the Moorish rulers of Ronda, and later was said to have been the residence of **King Ferdinand and Queen Isabella** after they conquered the town in 1485.
The palace is now the **Municipal Museum,** where visitors can learn about Ronda's history from the **Stone Age** to the present day.
The palace also features beautiful **Moorish Courtyards** with fountains and arches, lush gardens with exotic plants and flowers, and stunning views of the **Sierra de Grazalema Mountains** from its balconies and windows.

Granada:
At the foothills of the **Sierra Nevada Mountains.**
Alhambra - Palace and Fortress.
The Alhambra is a must visit.
There is so much to it and so many unexpected features in this sprawling fortress built in the mountains.
From many **Royal Palaces** and **Cool Patios** with **Reflecting Pools** from the **Nasrid dynasty** to the **Fountains and Orchards of the Generalife Gardens.**

There is a **Granada Card** that will get you free entrance to these sites and also free bus rides.

In addition to this, the card will get you into sites even when the tickets have all been sold out.

Visit **The Science Museum.**

There are numerous excellent restaurants here and a great night life with theatre and clubs.

Sierra Nevada - Mountain range in the **Andalusian Province** of **Granada.**

It is the highest point in the country with the mighty **Mulhacén** at 3,479 metres above sea level.

Known mainly as a ski resort but in the summer months there is hiking, mountain climbing and a whole host of other adventures to be had here.

If you are trekking here, watch out for:

Three types of **Squirrel:**

The Western Gray Squirrel

The Douglas Squirrel

And **The California Ground Squirrel**

Also:

The Lodgepole Chipmunk, Mountain Beaver, California Mountain Kingsnake, Black Bear, Wolverine, California Bighorn Sheep, Pacific Fisher, Mule Deer, and **Mountain Lion…. Grrr!**

Algeciras:

The last stop for those travelling further south and on to **Morocco** and **North Africa.**

There is no need to worry about buying last minute ferry tickets although you will see many street sellers hawking them on the roadside.

For good cheap ferry tickets to either **Cueta,** The Spanish enclave on the north African coast, or **Tangier** in **Morocco** and money exchange, look out for **Viajes Normandie.**

Follow the signs for the port/ferry.

Carlos runs the office with his daughter.
It is open 24 hours.
You will leave with cake and wine as a thankyou gift.

Carlos speaks good English, as well as other languages, and is extremely helpful.

https://www.facebook.com/Viajes-Normandie-sl-165074 7518519340/

The address:
Calle Fragata 3 Pol Ind Palmones, Algeciras, Spain

His office is two streets over from the **Lidls Supermarket.**

Look out for the **Camper Vans** parked up - lots of them.
- Parking Público Zona Comercial 4

If you need **Vehicle Insurance** it can be obtained easily at the Moroccan border.

North Africa:

Morocco:

Warm in the winter months.
Allowed to stay for 90 days with no visa
Not in Schengen or E.U..

Good time to tour: winter months.

Vehicle insurance and breakdown cover can easily be obtained from the office on the Moroccan side of the border.

Currency:

The Dirham is the unit of currency here.
It is subdivided into 100 Santimats.
Currently 13 Dirham are worth around £1.00.
Approximately 10 Dirham are worth 1 U.S. Dollar.

The peoples of Morocco Are extremely friendly, helpful and welcoming.

If arriving by ferry to the Spanish enclave of **Ceuta** the off loading and drive to the **Moroccan** border crossing can be a bit confusing and scary but try not to be stressed.
Ignore the chaos and keep calm, it normally works out o.k.

Places of interest:

A good touring route travelling from the north to south and back again - clockwise:

Tetouan -
Here there is a **Souk**, a **Medina**, and **El Hot Market** - Much cheaper than other tourist spots.

Camping friends of Cala Iris:
A Campsite worth visiting, on the foothills of **Cala Iris** (one of the few) - - amazing!!

Al Hoceima:
A busy seaside resort.
Excellent restaurants.

Al Hoceima National Park:
Climb or simply gaze at and enjoy **Cala Iris.**
The waters of this park are home to three varieties of dolphin, 69 species of birds.
Rays and sea turtles can also be seen here.
It is also home to pink flamingos and ospreys.
There are many treks and walking routes over this park.
Some amazing views.

Tazekka National Park:
Jebel Tazekka - Mountain in the Park
There is so much to wonder at here.
You will need a good week to explore the **Peaks** and the **Gorges**, the **Caves** and the **Lakes**.

Fez: One of the best large towns to visit. Not as commercialised or westernised as some.

Good place for shopping.

Hire a guide for the day to explore the amazing houses, shops, market stalls, restaurants and the maze of the **Medina**.

Errachidia:
Largish community speaking Berber and Arabic. Good centre for going on a tour.

Famous for its locality to various caves.

Merzouga Dunes:
A paved road from **Ouarzazate** gives access to the edge of the dunes, where many tour companies offer journeys by 4WD vehicles and by **Camelback**.

Tinghir - Todra Canyon.

Canyon Dades:
The best way to reach this spectacle of nature is by following the N10 route and travelling 110 kms south through **El Kelaa** and **Boumalne Dades** in **The Valley of Roses**.

Once in the gorge (spring is the best time), you will find gardens of palms, walnut, almond, poplar, and argan trees, and an incredible landscape for hiking, rafting, and rock climbing.

Ouarzazate:

Do not miss this great scenic route through to:

Zagora:
The Sahara here is a dry stone desert and less visited by tourists than those of **Merzouga** because there are no sand dunes.
However, the nearby beautiful sand dunes of **Erg Chigaga** are difficult to access.
To travel to **Erg Chigaga** dunes a 4x4 is needed.
In **Merzouga** you can visit the dunes with a simple car or bus.
That is not to say **Zagora** is not worth the visit.
The scenic drive from **Ouarzazate** is well worth the trip on its own merit.
It is the last large town before **Erg Chigaga** and a very useful stop for stocking up on essentials.
Zagora has a vast palm grove where over 30 types of date are grown.
There is an outstanding **Souk**, (one of the largest in Morocco) to wander around.
Watch out for the watermelons and colourful street art!!

Erg Chigaga:
Erg can mean sand sea or dune, sea or landform.
The **Erg Chigaga** dunes are 60 km southwest of **M'Hamid** and can be reached by a 4x4 vehicle in just a couple of hours, or 5 days there and back by **Camel** alone.

Oued Draa - Draa Valley - Algerian Border

Tantan:
A campsite on the Saharan border.

Guelmim:
The southernmost town and **Sahara Border** - watch out for the **Blue Men** of the Sahara.
Best **Camel Market,** also goats and sheep.
It is held on a Saturday.
Arrive in the morning.
On a Saturday, parking opposite the market is free.
Try tasting Chicken and chips in the market with **Harissa** (which is a very hot sauce).
Take the famous **Sahrawi Tea Ceremony.**
Buy a **Milfah.**
Visit the **Nomadic Museum** in **Tighmert.**

Camping is available at **Sidi Ifni, Guelmim** and **Tantan.**

Tiznit:
Excellent base for touring surrounding areas.
Just 45 minutes from **Agadir.**

Essaouira:
A bit of a detour but a great coastal port.
The best place in Morocco to watch the sunset.

Jebel Lekst:
Mountain (Lekst) - Ameln Valley:
Home to twenty-six villages each rich in cultivated green land and stunning backdrops of the **Jebel el Kest.**

The landscape around these villages is perfect for trekking, biking, or rock-climbing and a few of these worth mentioning are:

Oumesnat:
Home to **La Maison Traditionnelle** in which resides a Berber family teaching visitors about daily life there

Anameur:
The source of a natural spring

Tazoult:
Famous for its ancient **Jewish Cemetery** and **Jewish Silverware.**

Tagoudiche:
The highest village accessible by a rough track in a 4X4 vehicle.

Tirnmatmat:
Even further and more remote where **Prehistoric Rock Carvings** can be found.

The Ameln Valley:
Has the majestic **Jebel el Kest** as a backdrop, with gold and copper coloured terrain punctuated with patches of green cultivated land watered by springs and irrigation canals.
Did I mention that the valley has twenty-six villages?

Taroudant:

An **Old City** with a more gentle pace.
Great **Medina** which is less hectic, more leisurely.

Ouirgane valley:
Toubkal National Park and the quaint Berber Village of Ouirgane

Lalla Takerkoust - Takerkoust lake. Great for watersports and leisure!!

Ourika Valley:
Waterfalls - Beautiful valley.
Spring is the best time to visit but enjoy the **Saffron** (gold dust) harvest in November too.

Tichka pass - Tizi N Pass:
Breathtaking scenery and 'hold on to your knickers' roads.

Kasbah Ounila:
Well worth a visit.

Ait Benhaddou:
Amazing **Kasbah**. A fortified city built upon rock.

Marrakech:
A well known and frequently visited tourist hotspot.
Good base to travel and day trip from though.
Watch out for hoards of children following you.
Do not be tempted to submit to their pleas or to let them be your 'guide'.

Casablanca:
A port on the west coast.
A large town and business hub.
Some historical sites.

Rabat:
Contrary to popular belief, Rabat is the capital of Morocco.
It is a relatively quiet village or town.
The Royal Family spend most of the year here.
Rabat is considerably cheaper than Marrakech.

Africa:

It is not advised to cross the borders from Morocco to enter the disputed Sahara areas in the south or to enter Algeria in the east.

There are many seasoned travellers and local civilians who have journeyed along these routes without any issues whatsoever, however it would be irresponsible for us to advise the unprepared tourist to do so at present.

Tunisia is a relatively safe country to visit.

One must first cross **Algeria,** and again, further east, in order to access **Egypt,** one must travel through **Libya.**

The areas around the border crossings of **Algeria** and **Libya** are not thought to be safe areas at present and government advice is not to travel here.

Having said that, from **Egypt,** access to **Israel** is possible and also roads south as far as **South Africa** have been made passable……

This route would leave most of the continent of Africa open for road travel.

Thank you for looking and

Have an enjoyable journey.

The Middle East:

Israel:

Road Travel directly to Israel is not possible without some 'danger'.

Safeguards would be essential through **Syria** or **Iraq** in the north, or **Libya** in the west.
Algeria too may be difficult.

Access to **Israel** through neighbouring **Jordan** or **Egypt** is straightforward.
But getting to either country is difficult by road.

There may be a car ferry - *Visemar One*, which takes passengers and vehicles from **Venice**, in Italy, to **Alexandria**, in Egypt, a cruise which lasts approximately three days.

This service appears to be no longer running at the time of printing.

Once you have arrived in **Israel,** either by plane or passenger boat, car hire is available to visitors.

Israel is a place of some fantastic innovation and invention.
It is a country of creativity.

Currency:

The New Israel Shekel (NIS) is in use here.
There are 100 Agorot to each shekel.

A U.S. dollar is worth 3.6 Shekels
A pound sterling is worth 4.6 Shekels
A Euro is worth 4 Shekels

U.S. dollars can be exchanged for local currency.

Places of interest:

Almost too many to mention.
Grab a tour guide is the best plan.

Jerusalem:
The Capital City.
Visit **Masada National Park.**
The sites and sounds of **Jerusalem** can be, in many
ways, an emotional and evocative journey.
There will be guides to assist you in your journey here
and no doubt you will have your own plans and places
you wish to visit.

Jerusalem is the place where **Jesus** spent much time
and is where He completed His own purposeful journey
on earth before continuing with His **Father.**
Knowing what awaited him there, at the end of His
ministry, Jesus set his face towards going to the place
where He would give up His life.

North:

On the border with Lebanon:
Rosh Hanikra Caves.
Grottoes:
The power of the sea!
Take a **Cable Car** ride down the cliff face to explore these incredible formations.

Banias Nature Reserve:
Banias Waterfall:
The biggest waterfall in Israel.
Found in the **Upper Golan** between the fertile **Hula Valley** and the **Mount Hermon** mountain area.
Mount Hermon is the tallest mountain in Israel.

Galilee:
A good place for fishing.
The site of many miracles.
It was here that Jesus walked on water and calmed the storm.
It's where **John the Baptist** baptised **Jesus** and many others.
And it's where Jesus fed the masses with a few loaves of bread and fish and gave his **Sermon on the Mount.**
Jesus lived here for nearly thirty years.
The Galileans had a very noticeable accent which is partly why **Jesus's Disciples** were easily spotted.
The Mountains of Galilee are quite something to explore too.

A little further south is:

Jezreel Valley:
Mount Tabor:
The mountain upon which Jesus was transfigured.
Great for hiking.

Haifa:
Interesting and busy town with lots of terraces.
Especially amazing are the **Bahá'í Gardens** and **The German Quarter.**

Caesarea Nature Park:
A sea port.
There is a fantastic **Roman Amphitheatre.**
Also to be seen:
The Reef Palace
Archaeological Park
The Hippodrome Site:
A Hippodrome, reconstructed with **Frescoes** and an **Ancient Lavatory**
Bath House
Sea-Shore Promenade
The Old City and **Port**

The Valley of Elah:
David and Goliath battle scene.

The Dead Sea:
One of the desired tourist destinations.
Try to whip up a lather by soaping yourself in this lake.

The five **Cities of the Plain** that included Sodom and Gomorrah were situated in this valley before being destroyed.

Wadi Arugot, Ein Gedi
two roughly parallel canyons, **Wadi David** and **Wadi Arugot.**
There is a separate ticket office for each one.
Stick to the blue trail in **Wadi Arugot -** It takes about three hours.
Definitely avoid the red trail if you are with children but enjoy the **Fairy Pools.**
There are three hours of fantastic waterfalls and canyons here - definitely worth the walk.

Wadi David has several different routes, from one hour, to **David's Waterfall,** where you can take a swim, up to a full day's hike including **Shulamit's Spring, Dodim's Cave,** and finally, the **Ein Gedi Spring.**

At Ein Gedi, if you keep your eyes open, you can also see **The Nubian Ibex** - the biggest herds in Israel are here, **Wolves, Foxes, Bats** and **Birds of Prey.**

Timna Park:
The Negev Desert.
The site of thousands of mineshafts and the remains of copper smelting furnaces dating back to ancient Egyptian imperial times.

In the South:

Eilat:

On the Gulf of Aqaba - The Red Sea.

This is a busy **Sea Port.**

Eilat is a place full of activities and amazing things to see and do.

Here there is a **Dolphin Reef,** where the aquatic mammals are often spotted.

Known for snorkelling and diving, **Coral Beach Nature Reserve** has buoy-marked **Underwater Trails** among fish-filled reefs.

Coral World Underwater Observatory Marine Park has a glass-enclosed observation centre submerged offshore.

Here you will find a modern city filled with **Museums, Restaurants** and a busy city life.

20 minutes drive to **The Eilat Mountains** and **The Red Canyon**, which feels like a martian experience - very unusual scenery.

A very memorable trip!

There are many amazing and wonderful places to visit and things to do in **Israel**.

It is also useful to have a good working understanding of the Bible in order to achieve some perspective of the places you may visit.

Try not to get too wrapped up or overwhelmed with the commercialisation and religiosity of the places visited.

There is much to remind us here of the life of Jesus.

We can walk the streets that He walked and visit the places He visited and where many miracles were experienced.

The hill that He was crucified on and the area of the tomb, where, three days after He gave up His life, He was found to have overcome death.

We are able to imagine the type of buildings and areas where many hundreds of people were witness to His resurrection.

Jesus talked with His friends and disciples for 40 days after He was found to be alive, before He went back to His Father.

The truth is that the time of the birth, death and resurrection of Jesus is the centre and focus of all else that has occurred in the world, both before, in anticipation of the event, and since, in the changes that have occurred and are about to commence.

A visit to **Israel** is exciting and emotional.
It can also be busy and hot and dusty.

Whilst **Israel** is a great reminder for us of many spiritual aspects of life and death - a cornucopia of experiences and visual panoramas, it might be worth remembering that the tomb where Jesus was laid, is now empty.

He has risen and is no longer to be found in the physical land of **Israel** except amongst those who are His.

He is close to each one of us, wherever we may be travelling, in the world, and where we are right now, today.

His birth, life, death and resurrection were for one purpose only and that purpose was to destroy the curse that many of us still live under - sin and death.

His victory over death is an invitation for us to move out of that situation and into a new life - a life where we don't feel the need to be bad, to do harm, to be selfish, to please ourselves.

But we are pleased to, and able to, do things that are pleasant and healthy, to love and to live without the fear of death and without guilt for all time.

What Jesus achieved changed everything

Thank You.

The contributors to the first edition of this book are:

Rosselle Francis (aged 12).
See Pembroke Castle in Wales.

We look forward to there being many more names to add to this page.

Where to send your favourite places, ideas and additional information:

Tim Sweetman (the author) -
warwickhouse@mail.com

Tim has also written:

Journey Into Life:

What did Jesus really preach about when He was on earth?
Within "A Journey into Life" we discover the joy of travelling to a new place.

Tim has set our search for God's kingdom in the form of a journey to a new land.

Once inside the new land we begin a journey of discovery – everything is new.

Did Jesus teach that His kingdom is within our grasp?
Is this a land – A kingdom that we can live in now – in our own lifetime?

The answer is yes!

Some Adjustments Required?:

We live our lives from day to day carrying out regular routines and rituals often without thinking about what we do and what we say and why.

We take for granted that the things that we have done and said and even for centuries past must be correct because that is simply the way things are.

Tim has taken some of the many misunderstood concepts in the Christian life that we have, for so long, taken for granted and brought correction and redirection.

God is doing a new thing in this season and those who want to follow His direction need to hear Him.

A Time To Consider:

A Time to consider was written at a time when several friends and friends of friends had been taken Ill by potentially life threatening illnesses.

When this happens to us out of the blue it is naturally a shocking discovery to realise that we aren't going to live on this earth, in this body, forever.

It is however a reality that we all need to take into consideration.

Any of us may be taken away at any time.
Our life on earth is a very short period when we consider eternity.

Let us get involved with eternity now - we may not get another opportunity to do so.

The Shaking:

We live in a changing era.
God is moving and the earth is being shaken.
The church age is passing.
God's kingdom age is upon us.
How do the times that we live fit with God's plan for us in eternity?
Has our own past affected our present and will it affect our future?
Can we make an impact in our time?

Our Foundations:

Many of us have missed out on vital foundational truths in our walk with the Lord.
Consequently we tend to wander around unaware that we may be missing out on the good things that Father has planned for us, unsure of where we should be or what our purpose is here on earth.
As we look into "Our Foundations" some much needed clarity and understanding will be gleaned for our benefit and for that of the emerging kingdom.

Genesis part one:

There are many apparent mysteries for us to uncover when reading the book of Genesis.

In Genesis part one we attempt to uncover and give an answer to some of these mysteries.

We also invite the reader to consider the text for themselves and to appreciate that the Lord is wanting us to open up a discussion with Him.

Genesis part two:

In Genesis part two we continue to look at the line of progression that began with Adam and will continue to the birth of Jesus.

Noah has journeyed into a new era. Life has continued as the Lord promised.

Abraham, the man of faith and the father of all who choose to trust in Jesus, is born.

The nations begin to emerge from the mists.

Genesis part three:

Genesis part three brings us to the birth of Isaac who is a type of Jesus.

From Isaac, through Jacob, to Joseph and into the land of Egypt we can journey with the patriarchs and the children of the man who becomes Israel.

The Lord is bringing His plan of redemption to pass.

The End Times - For those who don't know Jesus:

The end times for non Christians spells out, in a relatively short book, the times that we are living in now and the part that non Christians have to play at the end of this age.

Entering Eternity Today:

Do we go to Heaven when we die?

For over two thousand years there has been some considerable misunderstanding and confusion with regards to God's kingdom.

Where it is taught, the question is inevitably raised, what is God's kingdom?
Is it a place we go to when we die?

Will we be taken there one day?
The answer to that one is a definite, no.

The enemy has been allowed to introduce an abundance of misleading teaching into the church circles that many of us inhabit in order to ensure that his kingdom remains.

When we uncover the truth of this deception and learn to live in God's promises he will flee like never before and the world will encounter a harvest unlike any other.

The Thief:

The basic beliefs and understandings of Christians are grounded in the interpretation of the scriptures that have been carried out by well meaning theologians.

But what happens to those basic foundations of truth when we discover that perhaps not all of those translations have been well made?

How great a part has the enemy of our faith played in the interpretation and representation of the scriptures that we read everyday in our Bibles?

We may find that we are living at a time when our understanding of scripture requires some adjustment if we are to enter into all that Father has in store for us.

Another Bump in the Road:

A tour guide into Europe, Asia, North Africa and The Middle East.

A book with a beginning but no end.

What began as a simple route planning exercise from the U.K. in the west, to Tajikistan in the east, which is as far as one can travel independently at this time, has exploded into an intimate guide to many other destinations.

The reader is invited to add their own pleasures and plans directly into the book on the pages provided and to also contribute to the next edition by sending their own experiences and enjoyment to the author for inclusion.

All contributors comments and contributions are to be added with a note of the contributors name and date of introduction - unless anonymity is preferred.